End of ai

WIDNES RLFC FROM THE 1987/88 UNTIL THE 1992/93 SEASON

Anthony J. Quinn

First published in the United Kingdom in 2019 by
The Cloister House Press

ISBN 978-1-909465-98-5

Also by Anthony J. Quinn

'The Greatest Try' – a book about former Widnes player Dennis O'Neill and Widnes RLFC Iin the late 1960s and early 1970s. 'The Words and Music of Anthony J. Quinn' - 20 songs that' can be downloaded or streamed on CD Baby, Deezer, Spotify, and most online digital music sites in addition to www.youtube.com. Two films 'Ditton Junction Remembered' and 'The Last Dance' are also on youtube.

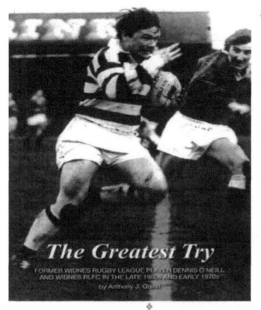

THE WORDS AND MUSIC OF ANTHONY J. QUINN

DITTON JUNCTION
Remembered

S.S. FISHER-MORE
'THE LAST DANCE'

*Written and presented
by
Anthony J. Quinn*

❖

*DVD Format
Running time 42 minutes approx*

❖

*DVD Format
Running time 1 hour approx*

Dedicated to John Quinn who played for Widnes in the early 1950s and who died in May 2017 following a needless tragic accident.

ACKNOWLEDGEMENTS

Colin Wright for prompting the writing of this book. Stephen Blease for allowing the borrowing of match programmes from the six seasons written about. Staff at Ditton and Widnes libraries, in particular Dean Allen. Reach PLC for allowing the reproduction of old copies of the Widnes Weekly News, Mike Flynn for allowing the use of photographs, Paul Haylett P-Tec Computers Widnes for scanning pictures and newspaper cuttings. Greg Oldfield Creative Design Widnes, for the front and back covers. Kym Holland proprietor of the Wellington Public House Widnes. Nigel Holland proprieter of Holland Chartered Accountants Widnes.

CONTENTS

1) "The emergence of a new great Widnes team"

Just over a decade ago I wrote a book which I titled *The Greatest Try*. The subject of the book was Widnes RLFC in the late 1960s and early 1970s. More specifically, it was about Dennis O'Neill, the team's brilliant young star of the era, who scored 'The Greatest Try' on his debut for Lancashire at the old Naughton Park in 1968. I was prompted to complete the book by life-long supporter of Widnes, and former workmate at Widnes Post Office Alan Mulqueen. I'm glad I did the book, but I thought after having completed it, never again! Writing a book is a long-drawn and painstaking process. I find it more concise and less time-consuming songwriting.

History repeated itself, and Colin Wright, a fellow musician and supporter of the Widnes Vikings, prompted me to put another book together about Widnes RLFC, making two alternative suggestions. They were to either write a book about the reign of 'The Cup Kings' from 1975 until 1984, or the brilliant Widnes teams of the late 1980s and early 1990s. I chose the latter suggestion for three reasons. Firstly, I did intimate in the last chapter of *The Greatest Try* that I would leave it to a better and more qualified writer than myself to write about the most successful era in the history of Widnes RLFC. Secondly, as already mentioned in regards to the expanse of writing a book, covering a period of six seasons from 1987/88 to 1992/93 was obviously going to be a lesser task than covering a period of a decade. Thirdly, whilst it was a privilege to be a Widnes supporter in the era of the 'Cup Kings', it was an even greater privilege to be a supporter in the late 1980s and early 1990s.

Note that I use the term "teams" of the late 1980s and early 1990s, rather than "team" of the late 1980s and early 1990s. This is because as in any era, there will be a turn-over in players every season. The change of players each season and during seasons before and up until the advent of Super League, was nowhere near as many. Six Widnes players were virtually first-team regulars in the seasons that this book is written about. They were centres Andy Currier and Darren Wright, the Hulme brothers David and Paul, forwards Kurt Sorensen and Richie Eyres. The incomparable Tony Myler and his often understudy at stand-off half Barry Dowd, were also in the first-team during this six-season period. However, Myler played in only a handful of games in the 1991/92 and 1992/93 seasons, and Dowd played in less than 20 games in three of them. Hooker Phil McKenzie never played in the first-team in the 1992/93 season despite being a key figure for most of the previous five seasons.

In contrast to the seven Challenge Cup Finals contested by the 'Cup Kings', only one was contested by a Widnes team in this era, Though not as successful as the 'Cup Kings' despite winning two Championships, three Premierships, one Lancashire Cup, one Regal Trophy and the World Club Championship, the teams of the late '80s and early '90s produced a magic that for me was unmatched by the 'Cup Kings'. In fact, I think they produced something that had never been matched by any team in the history of British Rugby League. Not even by the great Wigan sides of the era which were not only the 'Cup Kings' of the era, but were also Championship Kings. They won the Challenge Cup every year from 1988 until 1995, the Championship in 1987 and then every year from 1990 until the advent of Super League in 1996.

The two Championships won by Widnes were in the intervening 1987/88 and 1988/89 seasons. At the end of the 1988/89 season the Chemics as they were still called, were actually threatening to gain ascendancy over Wigan. They had won their second successive Championship by beating them in what was in effect a "decider" at Naughton Park in April 1989. One wonders if the Chemics had got through to the 1989 Challenge Cup Final, would they have defeated Wigan at Wembley also. It is hypothetical, but I tend to think they would have done. Of course, they never reached the 1989 Challenge Cup Final as they lost narrowly and controversially in the semi-final to St Helens. When I refer to the 'Cup Kings' of 1975-84 and the Widnes sides of 1987 until 1993, I should state that the intervening three seasons were not exactly disastrous.

They were only disappointing in the sense that the Widnes team never actually won a trophy. In the preceding 10 seasons at least one trophy had been won. They were though still "there or there abouts" in the mid '80s. In was in some respects a transition period, following the retirement of long-serving players like the late Mick Adams and Eric Hughes after the 1984 Challenge Cup Final. In the 1985/86 season the Widnes team still finished a creditable fifth in the old First Division, just three points behind eventual Champions Halifax. The following season the team reached the semi-final of the Challenge Cup, taking Halifax all the way before narrowly losing by 12 points to 8.

January 1986 saw the return as team-coach of the man who in my opinion was the key figure in the success of 'The Cup Kings'. I refer of course to 'Sir' Douglas Laughton. I think it is indisputable that Doug also moulded and produced the sides of the era that this book is detailing. In his second reign as team-coach, Doug signed many established Rugby Union players. In his book *A Dream Come True,* he explained that this was because it was not much costlier than signing untried amateur Rugby League players. Doug signed from Rugby Union Scottish international back Alan Tait, Rosslyn Park winger Martin Offiah, Tongan forward Emosi Koloto, Welsh international centre John Devereux and the most high-profile of all international Welsh fly-half Jonathan Davies. All of these signings more than made the grade in RL. Winger Brimah Kebbie and Welsh forward Paul Moriarity had less impact but were by no means failures. Kebbie's first-team opportunities were limited, whilst Moriarty was dogged with injuries.

Doug also signed Australian hooker Phil McKenzie from Rochdale whose role in the team I think was particularly significant. It was significant in the sense that running from the acting half-back position was becoming more prominent at the time, as a hooker's role in scrummaging was becoming less. McKenzie was often deadly in this role. Doug also made several astute signings of other experienced Rugby League forwards during the period. Notably Joe Grima from Swinton, Derek Pyke from Leigh and Les Holliday from Halifax. All of the aforementioned players blended perfectly with players who had come through the ranks at Widnes. The majestic and imperious Tony Myler, Andy Currier, the Hulme brothers David and Paul, the O'Neill brothers Mike and Steve. These local stars were at the Club at the time of Doug's return as was classy, pacey centre Darren Wright and rampaging second-row Richie Eyres.

All of the aforementioned players reached their peaks I believe in the late 1980s and early 1990s. And also, at the Club at the time of Doug's return was the most pivotal and important player of them all. I refer of course to New Zealand forward 'King' Kurt Sorensen. Whilst Currier, Offiah, Tait, Currier, Wright and co provided pace, mobility and spectacular tries aplenty, Kurt was leading from the front and doing the "hard yards". If King Kurt would have been an officer in World War One, he would have led his troops fearlessly over the top to the enemy's trenches. I doubt if any bullets would have stopped him.

It's hard to believe that Kurt was nearly 28-years of age when he signed for Widnes RLFC in the 1984/85 season. He was already a seasoned New Zealand international and is reputed to have said when he signed that he was "winding down his career". The King could not have known that he was to be the leader of the most exciting Widnes teams there ever was or likely to be. Nor that his achievements with Widnes RLFC would be the greatest of his illustrious career. He certainly "wound down" his career with a bang. He even scored a try in his last appearance for the Club in the 1993 Challenge Cup Final. The Chemics narrowly lost that 1993 final against the all-conquering Wigan team.

It really was the 'End of An Era' after that game. Widnes RLFC or Widnes Vikings have never been a force in British Rugby League since. Apart from the already mentioned three relatively unsuccessful seasons in the mid-1980s, a Widnes team won at least one trophy every season from the 1974/75 until the 1991/92 season. This is just one reason why I've titled this book *End of An Era*. Another reason is because I believe that even if a great Widnes Vikings team were to emerge in the future, there will never be anything quite like the late 1980s and early 1990s ever again.

I have also titled this book *End of An Era* because in 1993, it could not have been foreseen that British Rugby League would be transformed so radically with the advent of Super League within three years. Nor that those changes would affect Widnes Rugby League Club to such an extent. In an attempt to match Super League criteria, the Naughton Park ground was demolished, re-built and re-named. In truth, it needed updating irrespective of Super League. I'm not sure the iconic name of 'Naughton Park' should have been changed and updated as it were. The precedent of changing the first-team jersey each season was set along with the introduction of an away game kit. Also, the traditional and iconic nickname of the Chemics was abolished with the birth of the Widnes Vikings.

But what an end to an era those six seasons from 1987/88 to 1992/93 were. The following chapters will I hope give those who witnessed them a chance to re-live them. I also hope that younger, success-starved fans of the Widnes Vikings will gain an insight into the era, and perhaps what British Rugby League was like before Super League was born. In trying to fulfil these hopes, I have quoted in this book many descriptions of games by Dave Candler, Paul Cook and other journalists in the *Widnes Weekly News* during this period. My own personal descriptions are also after having read their match-reports at Widnes Library.

However, before I begin my chronicle of the six aforementioned seasons, I want to share my memories of the last game of the 1986/87 season. The Chemics had struggled to finish eighth in the old First division. Late in the season they briefly hovered dangerously near the relegation zone. This meant that they were to play champions Wigan away in the Premiership play-off first round. After years of mediocrity Wigan were back in business, winning the 1986/87 Championship by a country mile. It was a foretaste of what was to come from Wigan sides in the next decade. Prior to the game, Doug Laughton reputedly stated that the Chemics "had no chance". Doug may have been playing mind games as he often did, but most Widnes supporters would I feel have feared an end-of-season thrashing - I know I did.

A penalty-goal gave Widnes an early 2-0 lead, but it was soon cancelled out when Wigan's Kiwi centre Dean Bell romped through the Chemics defence for a converted try. The predicted hammering of the Widnes team by the Champions looked to have been set in motion. It was one-way traffic for the rest of the first-half, but it was towards the Wigan try-line. The inspiring Kurt Sorensen set up a riposte to Bell's effort try with a powerful break. In his last game for the Club, left-winger John Basnett finished off Sorensen's break for a converted try to put the Chemics 8-6 ahead. Another converted try by centre Darren Wright stretched the Chemics lead to 14-6. A further Widnes try was disallowed just before the interval. Had the Widnes gone in at the break 20-6 ahead, they may have pulled off a huge upset. The Widnes team eventually lost narrowly 18-22.

Wigan added the 1987 Premiership Trophy to their Championship by defeating Warrington in the final at Old Trafford. It was the first year it was held at the home of Manchester United FC. It has been held there ever since, evolving into the Super League Grand Final in 1998. Before the start of the 1987/88 season, Doug Laughton replaced left-winger John Basnett with a player who was to become one of the most prolific try-scorers and one of the biggest personalities Rugby League has ever known. He was to kick-start another five seasons of trophy-winning by the Chemics. Wigan were not going to have things entirely their own way in the foreseeable future. A great new Widnes team was about to emerge. One more exciting and flamboyant than the 'The Cup Kings'.

And no player was more exciting and flamboyant than the one Doug brought to Widnes in the summer of 1987.

UNLUCKY CHEMICS

Wigan 22pts
Widnes 18pts

The 1986-87 may now be over for the Chemics but if they continue to serve up the kind of rugby they provided at Wigan in Sunday's first round of the Stones Bitter Premiership Trophy then the next campaign should be one

Wigan given a run for their money

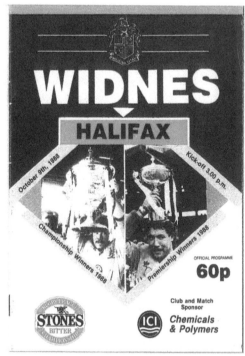

PROGRAMME SPONSOR TOTAL HEAT
Sunday, 16th September, 1990, Kick-off 3.00 p.m.
WIDNES v FEATHERSTONE R.

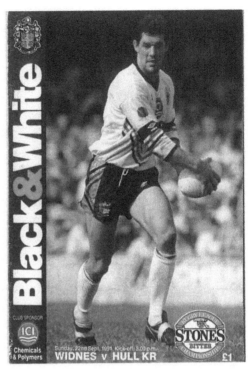

Sunday, 22nd Sept, 1991, Kick-off 3.00 p.m.
WIDNES v HULL KR   £1

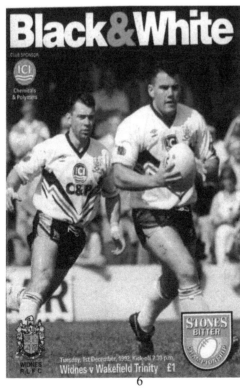

Tuesday, 1st December, 1992, Kick-off 7.30 p.m.
Widnes v Wakefield Trinity   £1

2) 1987/88 season "An uncoordinated clown"

The player I was referring to at the end of the last chapter was of course Martin Offiah. I stated in my previous book that younger readers would probably never have heard of Dennis O'Neill. Younger readers of this book I suspect have heard all about Martin Offiah. They may even have saw footage of some of his astounding try-scoring on the internet. Unlike Dennis, who I described as "The Legend That Never Was", Martin was most definitely a legend and still is. Heck, he's been awarded an MBE, appeared on *Come Dancing, I'm A Celebrity Get Me Out of Here'* and modelled in magazines amongst other things. For a Rugby League player to attain celebrity status you have to be something special, and he most certainly was very special indeed.

    The directors of St Helens in 1987 saw nothing special in Martin at all. The Saints coach at the time the inimitable Alex Murphy, wanted to sign Offiah, but was overruled by his superiors who thought that Martin was "an uncoordinated clown". They must have been drunk or smoked too much pot. Martin Offiah was just about the most coordinated, natural rugby player I ever watched. Tall, lithe, balanced and possessing unrivalled natural speed, he also had the ability to change speed at the right moment, an instinctive eye for a chance to score, uncanny anticipation for the bounce of a ball kicked ahead, marvellous hands and much more. In short, he was the Muhammad Ali of Rugby League. In his time at Widnes at least, he was like Ali in that he was a bit of a showman.

    He scored 181 tries in just 145 games for the Club and finished with a career total of 501 tries. The Widnes committee also had reservations about the signing of Offiah. It was the financial aspect of his signing that was apparently the stumbling block. It was perhaps understandable, given that the Club had lost over £26,000 in the 1986/87 season. Doug Laughton however was persuasive, and got the signing of Offiah sanctioned. Not only that, he obtained for Martin a 10-year contract. Doug had such belief in his signing from Rosslyn Park Rugby Union Club, that he was quoted in the June 17th edition of the *Widnes Weekly News (WWN)* as saying that Martin

"could become the best winger we've ever had at Naughton Park. I don't want to put any pressure on the lad but he really is something special. Give about six first team games and you'll see what I mean."

    Given Doug's prediction of the Widnes team's chances at Wigan in the final game of the 1986/87 season (even allowing that Doug was probably playing mind games), supporters would have had every right to be sceptical of his predictions about Martin Offiah. Also, the previous Widnes team-coach Eric Hughes, had made an extravagant prediction about a winger named Wilf George, who he had signed from Huddersfield. Hughes publicly stated he would be become an international. As it transpired, George just did not cut the mustard as it were, and was sold by Doug to Halifax within rag-time of him returning as first-team coach in early 1986. Laughton's prediction about Offiah was much nearer the mark, though not completely accurate. Martin not only became the best winger ever to play for Widnes, but arguably the best to ever to play either Rugby League or

Union. And as we shall see, it took just three, rather than six games to show he was "something special". The week following a pre-season friendly at St Helens, Widnes played their first league fixture of the 1987/88 season at home to Halifax on Sunday, August 30th. It had the ingredients of a tough opening game for the Chemics, as Halifax had won the Championship in 1986 and the Challenge Cup in 1987. Much of the attention was inevitably going to be focused on the performance of debutant Martin Offiah. Martin was actually down in the match-programme to play on the right-wing. Co-incidentally, so was the aforementioned Wilf George for Halifax. Both men played on the left-wing which was Wilf's regular position and was to become Martin's also. Wilf George had scored a try playing on the left-wing in the 1987 Challenge Cup Final. The Widnes team for Martin Offiah's debut consisted of three sets of brothers. It was:

John Myler, Duncan Platt, Barry Dowd, Darren Wright, Martin Offiah, Tony Myler, David Hulme, Kurt Sorensen, Phil McKenzie, Steve O'Neill, Mike O'Neill, Paul Hulme, Harry Pinner. Substitutes: Trevor Stockley and Richie Eyres.

A 5,300 crowd saw the Chemics start the new season in fine style with a 28-6 victory. Full-back John Myler kicked four goals and scrum-half David Hulme scored two tries, in addition to three others scored by forwards Kurt Sorensen and Mike O'Neill and right-winger Duncan Platt. Despite not scoring, the headline in the *WWN* match-report was **"MARTIN'S MAGIC"**. Offiah raised the cheers of the home supporters and impressed the match-reporter with some great defensive work. My own personal recollection of Martin Offiah's debut was of him spooning a pass from Tony Myler in a clumsy fashion when a try was beckoning. In the local *Hammers and Pincers* pub later in the evening, I expressed my reservations about Offiah. I opined to some fellow Widnes supporters that "he may be another Wilf George". In my life I've rarely got anything right about anything. The following week the Chemics won their first away league fixture by 18 points to 8 at Bradford on a rain-soaked pitch. Martin again did not score, but gave a hint of things to come with a scorching 60-yard run down the left-flank, evading three defenders.

Widnes players Paul Hulme and Harry Pinner tackle a Halifax opponent
in the opening league game of the 1987/88 season at Naughton Park.

The next game was also away on Sunday, September 13th. It was a "derby" just across the River Mersey against Second Division Runcorn in the first round of the Lancashire Cup. The Widnes team were hot favourites to win, but they were given a tough time in the first 25 minutes. They then scored four unconverted tries in the last 15 minutes before half-time, with David Hulme adding another brace to the two tries he scored against Halifax and were 16-2 in front at the interval.

Martin Offiah was still not "off the mark" as it were. That changed in the second-half, when he scored two great tries to equalise the couple scored by David Hulme in the first-half as the Chemics won in the end by 40 points to 6. I won't write "comfortably in the end" because the underdogs quite literally went down fighting. There was in the second-half a mid-pitch brawl involving 20 players. Just before the final hooter Runcorn's substitute back Tony Jackson - perhaps irked by Martin's two cracking tries - punched him in a tackle and became the second home-team player to be sent-off. The Widnes team however, were not completely sinless. Substitute Trevor Stockley was sent-off and second-row Richie Eyres was sin-binned. The following week's match-report in the *WWN* speculated on Offiah becoming a "folk hero". Praising the performances of both David Hulme and Martin Offiah it read:

"If this game threw up anything of consequence it was that David Hulme is in the best form of his life and could well be on the plane that is leaving for Australia at the end of the season and that Martin Offiah looks set to become some sort of folk hero. Hulme scored two tries, ran forcefully, backed up continually, and was easily the best player on the field.

Offiah also scored two tries in a manner that suggests he will score a lot more. He made his first out of nothing: twisting, turning past three defenders when it looked, he had nowhere to go. The second saw him weave through a shattered Runcorn defence to finish with a one-handed flourish. Needless to say, the crowd loved him."

The match-report conforms with my own personal memories of the Runcorn game. My initial doubts about Martin Offiah had been quickly dispelled! The report was also prophetic, David Hulme was selected for the 1988 Great Britain tour of Australia - as was Martin who most certainly did go on to score a lot more tries. In the same edition of the *WWN*, Doug Laughton's column was headlined **"Offiah the new Bev?"** - alluding to the great Australian winger Brian Bevan who scored 740 tries for Warrington between 1946 and 1962.

There was no stopping Martin once he had broken the ice at Runcorn. He proceeded to score at least one try in the next 14 games. Widnes were again in Yorkshire at Hull for their next league fixture, and as he did at Bradford, Offiah made another thrilling 60-yard run. This time it resulted in what was to become a trademark try. Stand-off half Tony Myler was at his majestic best in a 33-18 win. In his *WWN* column which was headlined **"Fans now have a team to be proud of,"** Doug Laughton stated that he went into his local in Newton-Le-Willows after the Hull game. He added, that he was told by some Wigan fans not to mention Offiah again! So, he proceeded to wax lyrical about Tony Myler's performance. Doug stated in his column that Tony was "some player" - which he most certainly was. He also praised the performance of hooker Phil McKenzie and highlighted that the victory at Hull was achieved without captain Kurt Sorensen.

On the Wednesday night after the win at Hull, the Chemics were away to another Second Division side Whitehaven in the next round of the Lancashire Cup. Although there was no repeat of the brawling and fisticuffs there had been at Runcorn, Widnes were given a tougher game than they had in the first round. The scores were level at half-time, and it was only an opportunist try scored in the 67th minute that sealed a hard-fought 20-14 victory. And of course, that try was scored by Offiah! adding to one he scored in the first-half. Doug Laughton must have found it was becoming increasingly difficult not to talk about Martin in his local. Back at Naughton Park on September 27th, the Chemics continued their unbeaten run with a comfortable 30-10 league victory over Hunslet.

The following Tuesday evening they were to face the mighty Wigan side in the semi-final of the Lancashire Cup. Wigan had also made an unbeaten start to the 1987/88 season. Not only that, they were on an unbeaten run of 25 games stretching back to the previous season. Whilst perhaps Doug Laughton's team was not quite "the finished article", the reigning Champions were not only a great unit, but had great individuals. Amongst others, they had scrum-half Andy Gregory and centre Joe Lydon, both of whom had originally played for Widnes. Wigan's biggest star though was loose-forward Ellery Hanley, who was voted the greatest British Rugby League player of all-time in 2007. Hanley was an all-rounder who played in various positions in his distinguished career. If Martin Offiah was the catalyst for the Widnes successes in the late 1980s and early 1990s, Hanley most certainly sparked Wigan's even greater successes in the same period. Leadership, strength, mobility, work-rate, defence, ball distribution, Hanley had everything. He was also a prolific try-scorer even when playing loose-forward. The Wigan Club more than re-cooped the world record £150,000 they paid Bradford for his signature in 1985.

Martin Offiah goes over for his first try for Widnes at Runcorn on September 13th 1987.

On paper at least, the Wigan side perhaps had the edge. So it proved, as Widnes were edged out in a pulsating game by 20 points to 12. Unlike the Premiership play-off game at Wigan at the end of the 1986/87 season, the Chemics never actually had the lead at any stage. They still showed they had enough potential to threaten Wigan's dominance in the foreseeable future. They only scored one try to their opponent's three, but it was the best of the game. It was of course Martin Offiah who scored it. The try was not an exciting individual effort, but it was an early glimpse of another aspect of his play. He would often come off his wing, and sweep unexpectedly into the attacking line in to finish off a move. This is what he did when Kurt Sorensen made a great first-half break. He also scored many tries through dogged determination, split-second quick-thinking and uncanny anticipation.

Martin was back in long-range trying scoring mode when the Chemics resumed their league fixtures at Salford after the Wigan defeat. He did though have to share the honours as it were with right-winger Rick Thackray and centre-partner Darren Wright. They both also scored after runs from over 50 yards. Whilst not as fast as Offiah, by ordinary standards Thackray and Wright were speedsters themselves. The tries scored by the trio were all converted by full-back John Myler as Widnes ran out 18-0 winners. A fortnight later on Sunday October 18th, the Chemics continued their unbeaten run with another decisive 32-8 home victory over Hull Kingston Rovers. The Chemics great table-topping form was not bringing in the crowds however. The week after the Hull Kingston game, Doug Laughton's column in the *WWN* was headlined **"Where are the fans?** Doug wrote:

"Arriving home after Sunday's win against Hull K.R, the wife asked: "What's up with the pan?" And words to the effect "Cheer up you're top of the league" What had depressed me about the match was the paltry attendance at Naughton Park of just over 3,000. Having been in the game for over 20 years, I know that all I had missing from the game against Rovers to make it a spectacle were the spectators to create an atmosphere.

What after all, is an entertainer without an audience, and more to the point what do I do now to eradicate this recurring problem? I accept the facts that we are a small town in a depressed area with high unemployment. The plusses are that we are now in the process of building a great side at Naughton Park. We have a wingman who is special and a crowd pleaser. We are an honest side and a good example to youngsters who are just starting to play Rugby League."

In retrospect, it is puzzling as to why attendances for home games in the first-half of the 1987/88 season were almost as low as in the 1967/68 season. Two decades earlier, in contrast to Doug Laughton's table-topping side, the Chemics were wallowing in mid-table mediocrity. Furthermore, as I also detailed in my previous book *The Greatest Try*, attendances at British Rugby League games in general were at a very low ebb in the late 1960s and early 1970s. In contrast, throughout the 1980s attendances in British RL were on a gradual upturn. Perhaps the Widnes people had been spoilt by the decade-long success of the 'Cup Kings'.

There was another sub- 4,000 attendance for the Chemics next home game against bottom-of-the-table Swinton. The form-book was turned upside down, as the Mancunian team inflicted on the Chemics their first league defeat of the season. In doing so and in complete contrast, the Swinton team achieved their first victory of the season. A late drop-goal by their second-row forward Les Holliday sealed a narrow, but deserved 21-20 win. Holliday was to sign for Widnes in 1990 and proved to be an astute signing by Doug Laughton. So too was Swinton's Kiwi forward Joe Grima, whose forceful running was a factor in their shock victory. Grima's display caught the eye of Laughton, who signed him within three months. Despite the defeat, there was no keeping that man Martin Offiah down. He scored two of the three Widnes tries and his personal "unbeaten" record since not scoring in his first two games, was to stay intact until the start of 1988.

The defeat against Swinton was the only league defeat prior to the new year. Six more league victories were reeled off through November and December, to consolidate the Chemics position at the top of the First Division. The first of these victories was a laboured 19-12 victory at Leigh. The *WWN's* match-reporter seemed to conclude from this hard-earned victory and the previous week's defeat against Swinton, that the Chemics were "unconvincing league leaders". Making his debut on the right-wing at Leigh was Australian utility-back Dale Shearer. A speed-merchant and an Australian international, Laughton signed him on a short-term contract. The following week he played at full-back in a 31-12 home victory over Castleford. Shearer not only scored a try, he also won the 'man-of-the-match' award. Doug hyped up Shearer in in his *WWN* column urging absent Widnes fans to "come and see him". There was even speculation that Shearer was as "fast as Offiah".

Dale Shearer indeed oozed class and speed, but there was no way he could upstage the irrepressible Martin Offiah. Martin scored another scorching 60-yarder in the next game, a first round John Player Cup tie away at St Helens. The game played on Saturday, November 14th was televised, and perhaps introduced Offiah to a national audience. It was only a consolation try in the last minute of the game, as Widnes went out of the competition by 12 points to 10. The game was effectively lost nine minutes from time, when the Chemics former Saints loose-forward Harry Pinner, threw out a pass that was intercepted by St Helens left-centre Mark Elia. Elia in turn fed his winger Les Quirk for what transpired to be the decisive try.

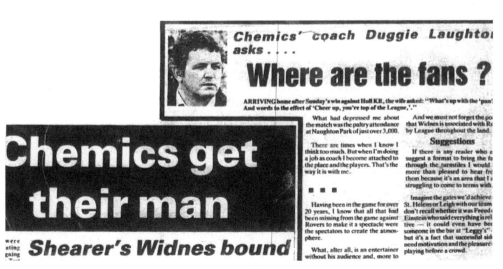

Martin scored two more when league fixtures resumed at Halifax a fortnight later, including another long-range effort in a 19-2 victory. And **"Offiah saves the day"** was the headline for the match-report of the 26-22 win over Hull at home the following week. In the December 10th edition of the *WWN*, part of the report read:

"It's becoming old hat to talk about Martin Offiah, but once again he was the inspiration for victory scoring two tries himself and setting up one for Mike O'Neill. Should he never play for Widnes again - unlikely I know - he is already assured of a place in local Rugby League folklore."

Perhaps because it was becoming "old hat" to talk about Martin, was the reason he did not get the headlines for the report on the home win over Warrington on December 27th. He ought to have done, as he again scored another 60-yard try - this time an interception - 10 minutes from time to give Widnes a narrow 20-17 victory. He had earlier scored a try which was a simple effort from close range. Dale Shearer also scored a thrilling second-half try made for him by inspirational scrum-half David Hulme. Hulme made a break from a scrum on the Widnes 25, raced some 30 yards before switching the ball inside to Shearer who raced another 40 yards to the posts. David himself had scored the opening Widnes try, when in complete contrast, he finished off a thrilling break by centre Andy Currier. Though he scored the first and made the third Widnes tries, David Hulme received a head-butt from Warrington forward Mike Gregory in the 36th minute who was promptly sent-off. Six minutes into the second-half, Kurt Sorensen followed Gregory to the dressing room for a high tackle on Warrington forward Gary Sanderson.

In between the hard-fought home victories over Hull and Warrington, the Chemics ruthlessly avenged their shock defeat at home by Swinton. They hammered the Mancunians by 52 points to 12 in the away fixture. Fifty-point totals were much rarer in the pre-Super League era. I attended this game and recall listening to Swinton's coach the late Peter Smethurst on *Radio Manchester* when I got home. He seemed distraught with his team's performance. He stated that in all his years in Rugby League he'd never felt so ashamed - or words to that effect. He also complained that Kurt Sorensen was allowed to swat off defenders with ease for the opening try. Kurt scored another one later in the game and hooker Phil McKenzie also grabbed a couple. Five more Widnes players also scored tries, the others being right-winger Rick Thackray, Dale Shearer, the Hulme brothers and of course Martin Offiah.

The victory over Warrington gave Widnes a seven-point gap as Division One league leaders. As already stated, the headline of the *WWN* match-report did not refer to Martin Offiah, instead it read: **"CHAMPIONSHIP FEELING!"**. There was perhaps, less than a Championship feeling after the first game of 1988 away at St Helens on January 2nd. The Chemics did not lose narrowly to the Saints has they had done in the John Player Cup in November, they were hammered. Not only was there no Martin Offiah try for the first time in 15 games, there was a not a try or goal by any Widnes player as they lost by 25 points to nil. Saints Welsh forward Stuart Evans had a great game, his powerful running constantly made inroads into the Chemics defence. The headline of Doug Laughton's column in the *WWN* was none the less '**88 – a year of great expectatations**' Doug began: "To say the least, we started the year on a poor note." But further wrote:

"Enough of that. One game does not make or break a season. I'm still pleased with the way the side's progressing and if we refer back to the Warrington game at Christmas what a treat that was.

Over the past five years of Widnes-Warrington games the top attendance is around 6,200, but a fortnight ago it was nearly 11,000. With Wigan and Leeds still to visit Naughton Park, the future of the club looks rosy. We can confidently expect our average gate to top the 5,000 mark which might even make a profit as well as winning something for the first since my return to Naughton Park."

Attendances were gradually increasing at Naughton Park since Doug had asked "where are the crowds?" back in October. There was a 5,000 plus attendance at Naughton Park ground when lowly Leigh were the visitors to Naughton Park on Sunday January 10th. The Division One leaders gained another two valuable points with a 14-8 win. Offiah - who had been selected for the Great Britain team to play France a fortnight hence - resumed his try-scoring after his blank at St Helens. Full-back Duncan Platt also scored a try, but it was hooker Phil McKenzie's effort which was the best and the match-clincher. The score had been locked at 8-8 for half-an-hour when McKenzie darted typically from acting half-back late on to score the winning try. The game marked the debut of Joe Grima, who had now been signed from Swinton. Grima was one the substitutes and replaced second-row Steve O'Neill at half-time. Whilst Grima was starting his time at Widnes, loose-forward Harry Pinner's time at the Club came to a sudden end. Derek Pyke, Leigh's prop-forward also played his last game for his club. The two players were exchanged in a secret deal before the game! The Leigh Club received a £50,000 cash adjustment.

WIDNES — FIRST DIVISION LEADERS — JANUARY 1988

Pyke made his Widnes debut the following week at Leeds. Despite a 21-26 defeat, the headline in the *WWN* report was **"THIS IS WHAT CHAMPS ARE MADE OF"**. Even Doug Laughton stated in his weekly column "What a tremendous game that was". From a neutral point of view, it was indeed a tremendous game between two teams chasing the Championship. Full-back John Myler dropped an early goal to give the Widnes team a single point advantage. The Headingley outfit then stormed into a 16-1 lead after half-an-hour. With 20 minutes left, the Chemics had roared back to lead 21-18 through two converted tries by Richie Eyres and a cracker from Aussie Dale Shearer. Shearer raced 60 yards after right-winger Rick Thackray kicked on when Leeds dropped a pass in the Widnes 25. Thackray re-gathered the ball and fed the Australian who sped away to the posts. The Leeds team though had the last say, scoring eight late points to claim victory.

Dale Shearer played at stand-off in the Headingly thriller. It was one of three positions he covered in his short spell at the Club. He was speed, class and versatility personified. He also took up the mantle of goal-kicker in a few games. One of those games was in the next home fixture against Salford on January 24th. He converted three of the four Widnes tries in a 22-2 victory. The four tries were shared by Andy Currier - playing this game on the left-wing in place of the on international duty Offiah - and Richie Eyres adding to the couple he scored at Leeds. The start of the match-report in the *WWN* read:

"Young guns Andy Currier and Richie Eyres collected two tries each as the Chemics took another major step towards the 1988 Stones Bitter RL Championship title on Sunday. Currier emerged from the awesome shadow of Martin Offiah to show the former Rosslyn Park RU wonder kid he's not the only speed merchant able to set pulses racing at Naughton Park.

And loose forward Eyres once more demonstrated his knack for taking the half-chance to rack up four tries in eight days, following his two scores at Leeds the previous Sunday."

Offiah was back on the left-wing the following week, as the Chemics began their Challenge Cup campaign at Dewsbury. Inevitably almost, he scored two of the seven Widnes tries as the Second Division side were easily beaten 38-10. The Chemics were drawn away to another Yorkshire Second Division team Keighley, in the next round. They proved a tougher nut to crack than Dewsbury, but the Chemics progressed with a 16-2 victory. Right-winger Rick Thackray scored two fine tries, Dale Shearer also scored a try and won another man-of-the-match award in his last game for the Club. Prior to the Keighley cup-tie, Doug Laughton had again been singing the praises of Shearer in his February 4th *WWN* column headlined **"There's only one Dale Shearer!"**. Doug stated that he would be in his "all-time greats side". He previously intimated that he wanted Shearer back for the following season.

Given the impending return of Shearer to Australia, and also the recurring injuries to Tony Myler, it was perhaps surprising that at the beginning of February 1988, stand-off half David Ruane was sold to Leigh. Ruane had played in nine games before he followed Harry Pinner out of the Club in a similar out-of-the-blue fashion. In between the two Challenge Cup games, the Chemics gained another decisive home victory over Bradford. There was another encouraging 5,000 plus gate for this game on February 7th. The *WWN's* match-reporter Dave Candler, may have stated that it was "Old Hat" to write about Martin Offiah. He either changed his mind or the editor of the newspaper thought otherwise. The headline of the report on the Bradford encounter was **"WONDER WINGER'S HAT-TRICK GLORY"**. Martin scored his first career hat-trick and his third try late on, brought the house down. Here is how is how it was described:

"Offiah left his most thrilling try to last as a lazy David Redfearn pass just outside the Widnes '25 went to ground. Offiah pounced and hoofed the ball upfield, hacked on again collecting it in front of Ford and completing the 70-yard move with a sensational touchdown that left the Widnes fans in raptures. John Myler's conversion from the touchline maintained the standard."

Doug Laughton's table-topping team were again to face Wigan in a home league fixture on February 21st, and away in the Challenge Cup third round the following Saturday. In the league game as in the Lancashire Cup semi-final, the Chemics lost narrowly, this time 12-16. Unfortunately, it was a mistake by full-back John Myler that resulted in the winning try by Wigan forward Andy Goodway. Half-back Shaun Edwards knocked the ball out of Myler's hands near the Widnes line, it was passed on to Goodway who sealed the victory for the visitors. In the previous home against Bradford, despite Martin Offiah getting the headlines and his first hat-trick of tries, John Myler had won the man-of-the-match award with a display described in the match-report as "rock steady". If not as gifted as brother Tony (who was?) John Myler was a fine player and in his testimonial year at Widnes.

Offiah the Great

CHEMICS' living legend Frank Myler this week paid tribute to wing sensation Martin Offiah - the man who is poised to succeed him as the club's top try-scorer.

He set the Naughton Park record for the most touchdowns in a season back in 1958-59 when stormed in for 34 tries.

Frank, one of Widnes' all-time greats, knows that his reign is about to end with the the former Rosslyn Park Rugby Union ace was even more puzzling, since Offiah had scored on his debut against the French at Avignon a fortnight playercthat people want to pay to watch. There's no finer sight than a wingman in full flight. Widnes are fortunate to have signed him'.

Unfortunately, Myler made another error that was instrumental in the Widnes team losing the Challenge Cup game also. Twenty minutes from time, he fumbled an awkwardly rolling ball and knocked on just yards from the Widnes line. Wigan won the ensuing scrum, and the ball was swept quickly out to their Kiwi left-winger Tony Iro who scored in the corner. Completely against the run-of-play, Wigan had a 4-1 advantage - John Myler had dropped a goal in the first-half for Widnes. HOWEVER, it was bad luck and perhaps bad refereeing rather than Myler's error that was the Chemics downfall. The game was televised and Ray French stated in his BBC commentary "Widnes hammered the Wigan line for an hour". In that hour the Chemics were easily the better side, but just could not score. They got over the Wigan try-line twice in the second-half, but efforts by forwards Mike O'Neill and Richie Eyres - both finishing off brilliant passing moves - were controversially disallowed. Wigan full-back Steve Hampson who had created the overlap for Wigan's first try, scored a second near the end and the daylight robbery was complete. The final 10-1 scoreline in Wigan's favour was unusual and definitely unjust. Doug Laughton began his column in the *WWN* the following Thursday stating:

"No doubt like myself and everyone down at Naughton Park, you supporters are feeling cheated after Saturday's Cup defeat at Wigan. We can all accept the run of the ball and bad luck going against us but to score what were two perfectly good tries and have them taken away leaves a bad feeling."

There was such bad feeling that Jack Ashley MP wrote an additional letter to one sent by the Club to the League Headquarters, protesting about the match-referee and linesman. Both the Club and Ashley, requested that the officials be not appointed to games involving Widnes in the future. Irrespective of the injustice of the Chemics Challenge Cup exit, the luckless John Myler was dropped when the League Championship campaign resumed with an away game at Hull Kingston Rovers on March 13th. Doug Laughton gave a debut to 18-year old David Marsh. The full-back curse continued as the teenager dropped a high kick resulting in a Rovers try. It proved to be costly as Myler's mistakes in the Wigan games as a narrow 10-14 defeat was incurred. Both Widnes tries were scored by Martin Offiah who had not scored in the two Wigan games or in the preceding cup-tie at Keighley.

Almost as if determined to make up for his three-game drought, Martin scored a second-half hat-trick in the next week's home game to Leeds in which Duncan Platt was selected at full-back. When scoring one from inside his own half, Martin teased some chasing Leeds defenders by showing them the ball as if to say "catch me if you can". Needless to say, the Leeds team were not pleased. The ensuing kick-off from the try was directed to Offiah's wing and a Leeds "reception committee" waited for him! Doubtless pleased with a superb 32-6 victory, and Martin's tries, Doug Laughton was less pleased with his showboating. He stated in the *WWN:*

"After Sunday's victory over Leeds I went straight to Martin Offiah in the dressing room and said: 'I'm going to tell you this once and once only. Put the ball over the line before you start the antics. What worried me was that minutes after the ncident two Leeds players had hold of him and a third came in and nearly broke his back. That, I would term, learning the hard way."

The evening prior to Doug's column, Martin scored a significant try in a mid-week game at Castleford. It was one that equalled Frank Myler's season's try-scoring record for the Club of 34 set in the 1958/59 season. It was centre Andy Currier however, who set the record total for tries in an individual game for the season at Castleford. He scored four tries in a victory even more emphatic than the one over Leeds. The 39-6 scoreline suggested Widnes were in form to take revenge in the away league fixture at Wigan at the weekend. It was the apt game for Martin Offiah to go past Frank Myler's record. It was also an opportunity to avenge the injustice of the Challenge Cup game. There was no Offiah try and there was no revenge. There was no injustice in this game either. Widnes were well beaten 28-2 by a Wigan team not giving up their Championship crown easily. The Chemics own Championship hopes were dented in the process. St Helens after a slow start to the season, had edged to the top of the league after 12 successive victories. They were now top on points difference and also had a game in hand over Widnes entering the Easter period at the start of April.

Shaking off the defeat at Wigan, the Chemics inflicted their third 30-point thrashing in their last four games at Warrington on Good Friday. In contrast to the Saints, the "Wires" had slipped out of the Championship race. I recall the cheers of Widnes fans leaving 'Wilderspool stadium, when news filtered through that Wigan had won at St Helens. The Chemics were now to face the Saints at Naughton Park on Easter Monday holding a two-point advantage at the top of the division. With only one away game at relegated Hunslet to follow, victory over St Helens though not certainly, would virtually win the Championship.

JACK BACKS CLUB

By David Candler

JACK Ashley MP has added his voice to the protest over the Chemics' controversial exit from the Silk Cut Challenge Cup. Widnes-born Mr. Ashley, who is now the Labour Member of Parliament for Stoke South, has written a strongly worded letter of support to the Rugby League Club, saying

having what club chairman Ray Owen described as two "perfect" tries disallowed. The matter was being dealt with by League officials in Leeds yesterday afternoon (Wednesday).

Mr Ashley's letter from the House of Commons was among many other letters and phone calls received by both Widnes and the Rugby League - all in support of the protest.

Indeed, the League were so inundated with calls last week that at one point they refused to take any more.

The Right Honourable Mr Ashley wrote: "At the weekend I read

of your protest at the handling of the Silk Cut Challenge Cup quarter-final game at Wigan and I am writing to say that I believe your indignation is fully justified and I strongly share it.

'SUPERB'

'I thought that your team was superb, showing great restraint and discipline and the deserved victory.

'It was a proud day for sport and although there is not much we can do about the official result - though there ought to be - you were right to express your deep concern. You deserve wide spread public support.

● Jack Ashley MP - right behind the Chemics.

End of an Era

Nearly 13,000 were on the Naughton Park terraces for the showdown Widnes put one hand on the Championship trophy by winning 16 points to 6. Even more so than in any previous game during the season, it was the Martin Offiah show. He scored all three Widnes tries and all resulted from great moves within the Widnes half. In his first and third tries he showed his handling skills and dexterity For his first try four minutes before half-time, he took a pass from David Hulme one-handed, before racing 20 yards to the posts after coming off his wing and linking up with the attack. His third try was the best of the three. Taking a pass from substitute forward Joe Grima inside the Widnes half a delayed change of pace and swerve took him past opposing winger Barry Ledger, he then kicked off the side of his left foot around full-back Phil Vievers, anticipated the bounce of the ball, re-gathered like a basketball player, touched down and was mobbed by ecstatic fans at the Sinclair Avenue end. Martin was chaired off the field at the end of the game. His three tries against St Helens took his season's total to 39. He had broken Frank Myler's Club record with the first of two tries at Warrington on Good Friday,

The Champions elect duly claimed their crown on Sunday April 10th at Elland Road, Leeds, which was the home ground of relegated Hunslet. It was appropriate that a 12-try extravaganza was served up in a 66-14 massacre of the Division Two bound Yorkshire outfit. It was also apt that try-scoring honours in the title-clinching game were shared out, in contrast to the St Helens encounter Martin Offiah scored another couple, but braces were also scored byright-winger Rick Thackray, right-centre Andy Currier, hooker Phil McKenzie and second-row Paul Hulme. David Hulme and the majestic Tony Myler - injured for much of the season - shared the other two tries. Even the conversions of nine of the tries were shared between stand-off Barry Dowd and full-back Duncan Patt. Dowd was substituted by Tony Myler at half-time.

It had indeed been a team effort throughout season. Widnes won the 1987/88 Championship finishing four points clear of St Helens and Wigan. They had won 20 and lost just six of their league games. Widnes captain Kurt Sorensen received the trophy and the team did a lap of honour to cheers from traveling supporters. Without digressing into knocking so-called 'Super League', isn't this how Championships should be won? Teams play each other home and away and which team accumulates the most points are Champions? No need for Grand Finals or 'Grand Farces' as I call them. There were play-offs for the Championship prior to the re-introduction of two divisions in the 1973/74. But pre-1974 all the teams were in one league and apart from a few inter-county fixtures, clubs only played teams in their own counties in a season.

When two divisions were re-introduced, an end of season tournament was also introduced to replace the play-off for the Championship. In the 1974/75 season, the tournament was named 'The Premiership' and only involved the top eight teams in Division One. The Championship winners would play at home the team finishing eighth in the table, the runners-up would play the team finishing seventh and so on. It was a good formula in my opinion. It gave an opportunity to for the Championship winners to put icing on the cake as it were, and a chance for the other seven teams win a consolation prize.

1987/88

Widnes as the 1987/88 Champions were to play eighth-placed Halifax at home in the first round on Sunday April 18th. Though the Championship had been won, Doug Laughton was looking ahead and had signed from Scottish Rugby Union Alan Tait. Another speed-merchant, Tait as we shall see was to become an attacking full-back. Tait was a substitute for the Halifax game and came on in the second-half. The Chemics never looked in danger of losing and progressed to the semi-final with a 36-26 victory. As in the season's opening game at home to Halifax, scrum-half David Hulme scored two tries and displayed the form that won him selection for the forthcoming tour to Australia. Paul Hulme was also belatedly flown out to Australia play as hooker for Great Britain in the third Test. Both brothers played inspired roles in a 25-12 victory, although the series was lost as the Aussies had won the first two Tests.

Following the defeat of Halifax in the first round of the 1988 Premiership competition, the Chemics were to face the old enemy Warrington at Naughton Park in the semi-final. The "Wires", had finished sixth in the league table. In the first round they had surprisingly beaten third-placed Wigan away. In the match-programme it was written:

"Warrington have the little matter of a 6-35 thrashing at Wilderspool on Good Friday to avenge and will be going all out to reach Old Trafford. If they can recapture the aggression and commitment, they showed in their superb First Round win at Central Park then Widnes are in for a really gruelling afternoon."

Widnes Captain Kurt Sorensen lifts the 1988 Stones Bitter Championship Trophy.
Steve O'Neill hoisting the base.

The Warrington team certainly did show aggression and commitment as they went into a 10-0 lead in the opening half-hour. Sadly, the aggression that made the headline of not only the *WWN* match-report, but also the front-page story, was aggression on the terraces. Not only was there fighting on the terraces, it also spilled onto the pitch. Warrington's right-winger Des Drummond floored a Widnes spectator. The respective headlines were **"RL's DAY OF SHAME"** and **"BLACK DAY FOR SPORT"**. The violence was even reported in some national newspapers. In his *WWN* column Doug Laughton blamed the trouble on Warrington supporters. The Rugby League authorities took to a more neutral view, and both clubs were fined £3,000. As the violence subsided after half-time, the Chemics having drawn level, went on to a 20-10 victory. Ironically, it was the Chemics former Warrington right-winger Rick Thackray who was the match-winner. Not only did he score a cracking 40-yard try, but he also made for one for David Hulme.

Championship runners-up St Helens were to be the Chemics opponents in the 1988 Premiership Final at Old Trafford on Sunday May 14th. The venue for Premiership Final had been moved to the Manchester United football ground the year previously. It was a good, innovative idea by the Rugby League authorities that resulted in attendances for the finals to increase significantly. The attendance for the 1988 Premiership Final was 35,252. The Widnes team that opposed St Helens was:

Duncan Platt, Rick Thackray, Andy Currier, Darren Wright, Martin Offiah, Barry Dowd, David Hulme, Kurt Sorensen, Phil McKenzie, Joe Grima, Ste. O'Neill, Paul Hulme, Richie Eyres. Substitutes: Alan Tait and Mike O'Neill.

On a hot May afternoon, the Saints were never really in it. Widnes showed the class, speed, strength and teamwork that had made them Champions. After Kurt Sorensen wiped out an early St Helens penalty goal with a seventh-minute try, the Chemics were always in command. Scrum-half David Hulme and classy centre Darren Wright added further first-half tries to help Widnes to a 16-2 lead at the interval. Darren's was a belter, he threw an outrageous dummy from in his own half and his pace did the rest. The Chemics were equally as dominant in the second-half as a 38-14 rout was completed. Hulme and Wright also scored tries in the second-half, as did substitute Alan Tait and hooker Phil McKenzie. Doug Laughton's "new" Widnes team seemed to be getting better, faster and more free-scoring. The 30-point plus haul in the Premiership Final was their sixth in the last two months of the season. Almost double the total of 30-point plus hauls they had scored before March. It was to be a precedent for the 1988/89 season.

Having already signed the speedy Alan Tait from Scottish Rugby Union near the end of the 1987/88 season, Doug was to make another signing from Rugby Union in the summer of 1988, in his quest to dethrone Wigan as the major force in British Rugby League. Although Widnes were Champions and Premiership Trophy winners, they had lost all four of the season's encounters against Wigan. Also, the Wigan Club were attracting the largest attendances. In order to counter this, in January 1989 Doug was to make yet another signing from Rugby Union. Unlike Martin Offiah, he was not a "gamble" as such, he was the biggest and most famous name in either code. Martin's ending to the 1987/88 season was actually something of an anti-climax. He finished as he started the season by not scoring in the last two games. He did not though do so badly in between. Not only was he the league's leading try-scorer, he also won British Rugby League's 'Man of Steel' award for the 1987/88 season.

And as we shall see, if the three tries "the uncoordinated clown" scored on Easter Monday in the crucial game against St Helens are part of his legend, they were almost insignificant in comparison to the hat-trick he was to score in a game at Naughton Park that was to decide the 1988/89 Championship.

The 1988 Premiership Final at Old Trafford: Martin Offiah and David Hulme
watch Phil McKenzie being tackled by two St Helens defenders.

Fixtures, results, attendances and points scorers 1987/88 season

Opposition	Venue	Result	Attend.	Goals	Tries
AUGUST					
30 Halifax	Home	28- 6	5,818	J. Myler (4)	D. Hulme (2). Sorensen, M. O'Neill, Platt
SEPTEMBER					
6 Bradford Northern	Away	18- 8	3,091	J. Myler (3)	Platt, Dowd, McKenzie
13 Runcorn (Lancashire Cup 1)	Away	40- 6	2,679	J. Myler (6)	D. Hulme (2), Offiah (2), T. Myler, J. Myler, Wright
20 Hull	Away	33-18	4,576	J. Myler (4). dg	T. Myler (2), Wright, D. Hulme, Offiah, Dowd
24 Whitehaven (Lancashire Cup 2)	Away	20-14	3,152	J. Myler (4)	Offiah (2), Platt
27 Hunslet	Home	30-10	3,612	**J. Myler (5)**	**D. Hulme, T. Myler, Wright, Offiah, Ruane**
30 Wigan (Lancashire Cup semi)	Home	12-20	7,306	J. Myler (4)	Offiah
OCTOBER					
4 Salford	Away	18- 0	4,190	J. Myler (3)	Offiah, Wright, Thackray
18 Hull Kingston Rovers	Home	32- 8	3,612	J. Myler (4)	**Ruane (2), M. O'Neill (2), Wright, Offiah**
25 Swinton	Home	20-21	3,877	J. Myler (4)	Offiah (2), McKenzie
NOVEMBER					
1 Leigh.	Away	19-12	3,971	J. Myler (3) dg	Offiah, Ruane, Sorensen
8 Castleford	Home	31-12	4,172	**Dowd (5) dg**	**Offiah (2), Sorensen, Wright, Thackray**
14 St Helens (John Player 1)	Away	10-12	7,322	Dowd	Sorensen, Offiah
29 Halifax	Away	19- 4	5,818	Dowd	Offiah (2), T. Myer, P. Hulme
DECEMBER					
6 Hull	Home	26-22	4,042	**Dowd (5)**	**Offiah (2), M. O'Neill, Thackray**
13 Swinton	Away	52-12	2,781	Shearer (7), Dowd	Sorensen (2), McKenzie (2), Thackray, D. Hulme, Shearer, Offiah, P. Hulme
27 Warrington	Home	20-17	10,755	Currier, Shearer	Offiah (2), D. Hulme, Shearer
JANUARY					
3 St Helens.	Away	0-25	12,978		
10 Leigh	Home	14- 8	5,100	J. Myler	**Platt, Offiah, McKenzie**
17 Leeds	Away	21-26	12,439	J. Myler (4) dg	Eyres (2), Shearer
24 Salford	Home	22- 2	4,698	Shearer (3)	**Eyres (2), Currier (2)**
31 Dewsbury (Challenge Cup 1)	Away	38-10	1,980	J. Myler (5)	Offiah (2), Wright, T. Myler, Shearer, D. Hulme, McKenzie
FEBRUARY					
7 Bradford Northern	Home	26- 4	5,096	J. Myler (3)	**Offiah (3), P. Hulme, J. Myler**
14 Keighley (Challenge Cup 2)	Away	16- 2	3,331		Thackray (2), D. Hulme, Shearer
21 Wigan	Home	12-16	12,147	J. Myler (2)	**McKenzie, Grima**
27 Wigan (Challenge Cup 3)	Away	1-10	18,079	J. Myler dg	
MARCH					
13 Hull Kingston Rovers	Away	10-14	3,568		Offiah (2)
20 Leeds	Home	28- 6	5,552	**Platt (4)**	**Offiah (3), Wright, Thackray, Currier**
23 Castleford	Away	39- 6	3,504	Platt (5) dg	Currier (4), Offiah, Eyres, McKenzie
27 Wigan	Away	2-28	14,236	Platt	
APRIL					
1 Warrington	Away	35- 6	6,836	Platt (5) dg	P. Hulme (2), Offiah (2), Currier, Thackray
4 St Helens	Home	16- 6	12,904	Platt, Dowd	**Offiah (3)**
10 Hunslet	Away	66-14	4,552	Dowd (5), Platt (4)	P Hulme (2), Currier (2), Thackray (2), McKenzie (2), Offiah (2), D. Hulme, T. Myler
17 Halifax (Premiership 1)	Home	36-26	7,679	Platt (6)	**D. Hulme (2), Eyres, Wright, McKenzie, Offiah**
MAY					
8 Warrington (Premiership 2)	Home	20-10	10,343	Platt (4)	Thackray, Currier, D. Hulme,
15 St Helens (Premiership Final)	Manchester	38-14	35,252	Currier (4), Platt	Wright (2), D. Hulme (2), Sorensen, Tait, McKenzie

23

Players total number of games and points 1987/88 season

	Played	Goals	Tries	Points
Andy Currier	17	5	11	54
Barry Dowd	30	(1dg) 21	2	49
Richie Eyres	34		6	24
Ian Gormley	1			0
Joe Grima	14		1	4
David Hulme	33		16	64
Paul Hulme	35		7	28
Ralph Linton	3			0
Chris Lloyd	1			0
David Marsh	3			0
Phil McKenzie	35		12	48
John Myler	21	(4dgs) 59	2	130
Tony Myler	14		7	28
Keith Newton	2			0
Mike O'Neill	36		4	16
Steve O.Neill	33			0
Martin Offiah	35		42	168
Harry Pinner	12			0
Duncan Platt	16	(2dgs) 31	4	80
Derek Pyke	11			0
Dale Shearer	14	11	6	46
Kurt Sorensen	32		6	24
Trevor Stockley	6			0
Andy Sullivan	5			0
Alan Tait	3		1	4
Rick Thackray	29		11	44
Darren Wright	33		11	44

First Division	Games	Won	Drawn	Lost	For	Against	Points
Widnes	26	20	0	6	641	311	40
St Helens	26	18	0	8	672	337	36
Wigan	26	17	2	7	621	327	36
Bradford Northern	26	18	0	8	528	304	36
Leeds	26	15	3	8	527	450	33
Warrington	26	14	2	10	531	416	30
Castleford	26	13	0	13	505	559	26
Halifax	26	12	0	14	499	437	24
Hull Kingston Rovers	26	11	1	14	420	480	23
Hull	26	11	0	15	364	595	22
Salford	26	10	0	16	368	561	20
Leigh	26	9	0	17	416	559	18
Swinton	26	4	2	20	390	780	10
Hunslet	26	4	2	20	363	779	10

3) 1988/89 season "First Division Champions again"

At the end of the triumphant 1987/88 season, Doug Laughton stated in the *WWN* there was "more to come". Despite the depth of talent at the Club and winning the Championship and Premiership Trophy the previous season, Doug had signed another winger from Rugby Union for the 1988/89 season. He also travelled to New Zealand in the summer of 1988 to sign a forward from Rugby Union who had been in the All Blacks squad. In his book *A Dream Come True* Laughton would describe winger Brimah Kebbie as one of his "minor signings". In contrast, he said of 23-year-old forward Emosi Koloto that had he have signed him when he was 19, he could have been "one of the best players ever". 'The Moose' as he was nicknamed by Widnes fans, was indeed a formidable player. Sixteen stone plus, six feet and four inches tall, mobile and again to quote Doug, Koloto had "magic hands". I also think that Kebbie was more than a "minor signing". He did a winger's business of scoring tries in his comparatively few appearances for the Club.

Koloto was not to arrive in England until October. In contrast, Brimah Kebbie was pictured in the July 31st edition of the *WWN* modelling the new team-kit for the 1988/89 season. It was only a minor modification of the black shorts and white jersey that had been worn since the early 1970s. For the coming season, the shoulders and arms of the jersey would also be black. In the modern era, the team jersey is often unrecognisable from one season to the next, and there are also ever-changing "away" kits. Kebbie also had a completely contrasting physique to Koloto. He was sleight, smallish, but wickedly fast and nicknamed "Little Martin" by supporters in his time at Widnes. Perhaps because of Offiah's sensational first season, great things were also expected of Kebbie. As in the 1987/88 season, the Chemics played a pre-season friendly at St Helens. Brimah did not play as the Widnes team incurred a 16-28 defeat. The *WWN* match-report in the August 18th edition was headlined **'NEW BOY ABSENT'** The report began:

"There were plenty of disgruntled Chemics fans around Knowsley Road on Sunday - disappointed not so much with the team's performance, but were to be denied a glimpse of the latest signing Brimah Kebbie. Kebbie signed by Widnes from Broughton Park Rugby Union Club at the end of last season, was scheduled to have at least half a game against Saints, and the prospect of his presence undoubtedly attracted many people to the game."

On Sunday August 21st, the Chemics had a more significant and symbolic friendly to play than the one at St Helens. As Champions they were to play the Challenge Cup winners Wigan for the Charity Shield in the Isle of Man. Widnes at last put one over the Central Park outfit. In a competitive game, Wigan dominated the early exchanges before Martin Offiah intervened. In the 20th minute Martin - who like Kebbie did not play at St Helens - in true Phil McKenzie style, went from the acting half-back position and raced 40 yards through the Wigan defence to give his team the initiative. McKenzie himself repeated the dose from an even longer distance in the second-half, as Widnes claimed the 1988 Charity Shield by 20 points to 16. Richie Eyres who played at loose-forward was quoted after the match as saying "At long last we've broken the jinx".

The Wigan jink may well have been broken, but the "business end of the season" was to start on Sunday 28th August. The term "business end of the season" is one that is used to describe the present-day Super League play-offs. I've used it sarcastically to have another knock at them as I did in the previous chapter. When the Championship used to be won by the team finishing top of the league, it was "business" from day one. The Chemics were to face Halifax in the first league game of the season as they did a year earlier. This time the game was away, and the Champions made a false start to their defence of the title. Before a 9,000 crowd, they lost 20-28 to the determined Yorkshire side. Halifax second-row forward Neil James claimed a hat-trick of tries and the man-of-the-match award. He did not however, score the try of the match. That was inevitably scored by Martin Offiah, who was certainly not making a false start to the season. In the 23rd minute he rounded three defenders in a scorching 70-yard run to the line.

After the false start against Halifax, Doug Laughton's speed-machine really roared into action in the next five games. Hull were the opposition in the first home game of the season on September 4th. Widnes supporters would have an opportunity to see Brimah Kebbie in action for the first time. The *WWN* preview of the game focused more on the return of Tony Myler. Kebbie kicked five goals and scored a try, but otherwise had a nervy debut. Myler who had not played a full first-team game since February was outstanding. The Maestro was man-of-the-match in an emphatic 38-6 win despite Martin Offiah's first four-try haul for the Club.

The following week another decisive victory was achieved at Leeds. It was though a late. late show that routed the Headingley outfit. The Chemics were trailing 12-14 with just 11 minutes remaining before Tait, Sorensen, McKenzie and Thackray went over for tries to seal a 30-12 win. Rick Thackray's try completed his hat-trick. So often overshadowed by the phenomenal Martin Offiah, "Slick Rick" stole the limelight for once. The fortunes of the right-winger had taken a turn for the better. Left out for the Hull game, Doug not only restored him in place of Brimah Kebbie, put selected him to play his first game for Lancashire against Yorkshire on Wednesday September 21st.

FIRST TEAM SQUAD BEFORE THE START OF THE 1988/89 SEASON

BACK ROW: John Stringer (secretary), Joe Grima, Richie Eyres, Rick Thackray, Martin Offiah. MIDDLE ROW: Vivian Gleave (physio), Derek Pyke, David Hulme, Paul Hulme, Barry Dowd, Mike O'Neill, Tony Myler, Andy Currier, Eddie McDonald (trainor). FRONT ROW SEATED: Alan Tait, Steve O'Neill, Kurt Sorensen, Phil McKenzie, Darren Wright.

The county game was also to be played at Headingley. Team-mates Derek Pyke, Darren Wright and Paul Hulme were also selected. One player conspicuously not selected was Martin Offiah, who had made his county debut the previous year, when in contrast to Thackray, he had not been a Rugby League player for a proverbial five minutes. Perhaps Doug was protecting himself against any accusations of nepotism. Or perhaps he had other sincere and ulterior motives!

You cannot though keep a good man down, and there was no keeping Martin Offiah down. After no selection for the county game and no try in the victory at Leeds, Martin scored two gems in the next game. In doing so he again made the headlines of the *WWN* match-report which read: "**OFFIAH MAGIC ENDS SAINTS COMEBACK**". Widnes defeated St Helens in the first round of the Lancashire Cup at Naughton Park. In contrast to the late, late show at Leeds, if it was not an early show against Saints, it was virtually a first-half show. The Chemics were 22-0 ahead at half-time and seemingly on course to hand out a real hammering. The Saints remarkably hauled back 14 points early in the second-half and got themselves within shooting distance of the previously rampant Widnes team.

In the 58th minute Offiah punctured any hopes of a remarkable St Helens come-back with his second try. When Widnes won a scrum just outside the Saints 25 and near the touchline, scrum-half David Hulme went to the blind side and fed Martin who shot between opposing winger Kevin McCormack and full-back Phil Vievers to put his team in the clear again. The final score was 32 points to 24. In his *WWN* column, Doug Laughton expressed his disappointment at St Helens being allowed to get back into the game. Even so, he was still taking pleasure from his team's performances. No doubt echoing the thoughts of most, if not all Widnes supporters, he stated in his column:

"I have watched the videos of our last two games against Saints and Leeds about five times each and when I see Tait coming into the line, Tony Myler sliding through, Wright and Currier stretching their legs and Martin and Rick on the wings, I rub my bad leg. I'd love to be able to turn back the clock and play with them."

Ten days later on the evening of September 28th, the Chemics swatted aside relegated Swinton in the second round of the Lancashire Cup. The Manchester team who had upset the odds the previous season at Naughton Park, were dispatched by 38 points to 4. It was the last of a five-game sequence in which Doug Laughton's team scored at least 30 points. In between the two Lancashire Cup games, the Chemics played a league game at home against Featherstone Rovers. The Chemics annihilated them by 58 points to 2. Martin Offiah went on another four-try spree, Andy Currier did even better and scored five, equalling the Club record for tries by a Widnes player in a game. Andy also kicked seven goals to break the existing Club record for points in a game by an individual player.

The month of October saw a lull in points-scoring and form in two of the four games Widnes played. Doug Laughton's speed-merchants were de-railed as they incurred their second league defeat of the season at Salford. They had their chances but went down 12-15. A thorn in the Chemics side and a key man in Salford's victory was centre Keith Bentley. A brilliant young talent at Widnes in the early 1980s as a left-winger, Bentley came back to haunt Doug Laughton who sold him in his first spell as team-coach. Dave Candler the *WWN* match-reporter made more of the absence of Kurt Sorensen in his report than Bentley's performance. He wrote:

"It took Widnes just three days to discover the truth that Kurt Sorensen remains the key figure in their bid to retain the championship title. Fiery Salford shattered the view of Naughton Park boss Duggie Laughton that Widnes can continue to thrive without their inspirational skipper."

Kurt was absent again the following week on October 9th in a low scoring 5-4 home win over Halifax. It was his replacement Steve O'Neill who dropped a last-minute goal to give the Chemics victory. It was to be his parting gift to the Club he had served so well since signing from Wigan in 1981. A fortnight later both Steve and John Myler were sold to Swinton. Only the week before Doug Laughton was reported to be furious about approaches from other clubs for the two players. Both had made over 200 first-team appearances, but they were no longer first-choice selections. Alan Tait signed at the back end of the previous season, was in great form at full-back, whilst Derek Pyke and Joe Grima signed in January 1988 were becoming cornerstones of the Widnes pack. Three nights later Steve O'Neill made his last appearance for the Club in the Lancashire Cup semi-final at Wigan. As in the previous year's tie at Naughton Park, the Chemics lost narrowly 10-14 in a thrilling game.

Before returning to Wigan for the away league fixture on November 6th, Doug Laughton's team got back to a more free-scoring mode by winning 28-14 at Wakefield. Classy centre Darren Wright grabbed a hat-trick of tries and the headlines of the *WWN* match-report. All of the high-speed Widnes three-quarters had now scored at least three tries in a game in the season to gain the headlines of respective match-reports. And now there was a speed-merchant at full-back in Scotsman Alan Tait behind them, and often linking up with the attack.

Martin Offiah in full cry for the line.

Richard Eyres breaks clear from a double tackle

Andy Currier on his way to a record, goes over for his fourth try.

Action from the home league game against Featherstone Rovers on September 25th 1988.

Prior to the league fixture at Wigan, Doug stated publicly that he thought he now had a better team than Wigan. His prediction that his Widnes team would win the league game was correct. Despite the try-scoring by the high-speed backs, Dave Candler once again stated that Kurt Sorensen was the key to the Chemics retaining the Championship. The King also scored one of the four Widnes tries in a vital 24-10 victory. Candler wrote:

"Sorensen's influence on this victory cannot be understated. He rose above the mindless taunts of Wigan fans with a splendid display of controlled aggression and was easily Widnes most impressive performer."

A letter signed by a "Season ticket holder" was published in the match-programme for the next league fixture at Naughton Park on November 20th against Hull Kingston Rovers. The Widnes fan concerned perceived the Wigan game differently and stated that Tony Myler was the best Widnes player at Wigan. He actually went further than that and wrote:

"For me one of the best features of the win at Wigan was the superb form of Tony Myler. He was brilliant and looked the best player on the pitch either with some creative attacking play or cast-iron defence. If he hadn't been troubled by injury so often, I think he would be recognised as an all-time great for there are few such 'natural' players around."

It was timely that Myler and Sorensen each scored two tries in the game against Hull Kingston Rovers. Martin Offiah also scored a brace as Rovers were thrashed 43-6. After a lean spell during October in which he did not score in three successive games, Martin had got back in the groove with a try in the victory at Wigan. In between the Wigan and Hull Kingston Rovers games, he scored another hat-trick when Featherstone Rovers returned to Naughton Park in the first round of the John Player Trophy. The Rovers contained the rampant Widnes try-scoring machine to 37 points this time around, and put 12 of their own on the scoreboard. Tongan Rugby Union forward Emosi Koloto at last made his home debut as a substitute in this game. It was Martin Offiah though who yet again got the headlines of the *WWN's* match-report which began:

"Emosi Kololo's long awaited home debut proved to be be merely a trailer the main event - the Martin Offiah show. And while Richie Eyres deservedly won the man of the match award with a non-stop running display and a part in three of the six tries, Offiah provided the headlines with yet another hat-trick."

Koloto was certainly going to be an addition to the "non-stop running" of Eyres. Widnes had now not only the fastest back-line in British RL, but the most mobile pack of forwards. The Chemics played Second Dvision Sheffield Eagles away in the second round of the John Player Trophy on November 30th. They predictably won by 32 points to 9, but it was not as easy as the scoreline suggests. As in the league game at Leeds, Doug Laughton's team cut loose late in the game with an avalanche of tries. Emosi Koloto coming on as a substitute again for the injured David Hulme, was among the five try-scorers. Widnes battled their way to the 1988/89 John Player Final on successive weeks following the win at Sheffield. I use the word 'battled' as the Chemics utilised their grit as well as their skill and speed to defeat Warrington at home in the third round and St Helens in the semi-final.

The games were played on the first Saturdays in December and were televised by the BBC.

Warrington played with fire and 150 per cent commitment in the first-half, and held a 6-0 advantage at the break. After half-time King Kurt and the Widnes forwards began to assert themselves. Koloto in particular, assisted Sorensen in the come-back. Another Martin Offiah special got Widnes back into the game early in the second-half. Taking a pass from Koloto on the half-way line, Offiah from a standing start, shot through the Warrington defence for a converted try to level the scores. The visitors edged ahead again through a drop-goal by their skilful half-back John Woods, but the Chemics prevailed by 16 points to 7 with two further converted tries. The first one was scored by hooker Phil McKenzie, who also laid on a second try in the last minute for Offiah.

Doug Laughton's team showed even greater resolve and grit in the semi-final played at Wigan the next week. Like the Warrington forwards, the St Helens pack threw everything at their opponents. The Saints were unfortunate to be 2-4 behind at the break. Unlike Warrington, they kept their momentum going and were 18-10 ahead with 15 minutes remaining. The Chemics went up another gear and stole a 20-18 victory with late converted tries by Andy Currier and Richie Eyres. With a place in the John Player Final sealed, the Chemics could get back to the business of retaining the Championship. Unlike the previous year, they had not yet hit top spot. Castleford had remained unbeaten having only dropped one point. Doug Laughton's column in the December 15th *WWN* edition was headlined **"WE WANT TOP SPOT BACK"**

The evening prior to Doug expressing his ambition, his team racked up another 40 points at Naughton Park as they defeated Wakefield Trinity. Given their great form, they seemed ready to do the double over Leeds at home at the weekend. Martin Offiah gave Widnes the initiative after 10 minutes with yet another 60-yarder, but the Chemics went down by 20 points to 8. Widnes were now three points behind the league leaders who had a game in hand. Doug Laughton's team were though about to launch an unbeaten league run of 10 games themselves.

Season's Greetings
To All Supporters
From Players
and Staff

The run started with repeat victories over Warrington on Boxing Day and St Helens at home on New Year's Day. As in the John Player Cup games, the victories were hard-earned. At Wilderspool the Chemics were 4-8 down at half-time before prevailing 18-8. The Saints again threatened to defeat the Chemics and were trailing by only two points, when a piece of Tony Myler genius put Offiah in for a decisive try. Tony was being bundled into touch, when he somehow managed an audacious reverse pass to Martin who did the rest. The final score was 29-22 in the Chemics favour. The headline of Dave Candler's match-report rather wryly read: **"MYLER HANDS SAINTS A NEW YEAR HANGOVER!"**

The headline of the front-page of the same January 5th 1989 edition of the *WWN* read **"CHEMICS GO FOR DAVIES"**. The article speculated that Widnes wanted to sign the brilliant Welsh Rugby Union fly-half Jonathan Davies. Davies was just about the biggest name in British, if not World Rugby Union. In a sense the headline contradicted what Doug Laughton had stated in his weekly column a fortnight earlier. Doug had intimated he would only announce signings when they were done and dusted. That seems to have been the case when Offiah, Tait and Koloto were signed. This was a policy in order not to disappoint the expectations of fans. As it happened, the Davies signing went through and the following week's front-page headline in the *WWN* was: **"HELLO CHEMICS"** which was accompanied by a picture of the Welsh Rugby Union star. An accompanying article read:

"A smile and a wave from Jonathan Davies that says I've no regrets. The Chemics prize capture from the Welsh Rugby Union was this week preparing to make his RL debut at Naughton Park following his sensational decision to switch codes.

Widnes coach Duggie Laughton scooped the Rugby League world when he persuaded Davies, the 26-year-old Llanelli fly-half and Welsh captain to join the league champions on a four-year contract with a three-year option. The undisclosed fee is believed to be worth around £150,000."

In my opinion, the Davies signing was one signing too many by Doug. Ultimately, he was too expensive and by 1993 the Club was in financial trouble and had to release Davies because of the size of his contract. I think Doug Laughton's calculation was that Davies would pay for himself. He didn't, and attendances only increased radically in the short-term. I take nothing away from the Welshman's playing abilities. He was a gifted player and always gave everything when he played for Widnes, producing many great performances. But as the saying goes "If it ain't broke, don't fix it". The team were flying and had great players in Tait at full back, Currier and Wright in the centres and Myler at stand-off. Many older Widnes supporters may disagree with my opinion. In the next chapter, I'll offer an even more contentious opinion as to why the Widnes teams of this era did not knock Wigan off their perch, and dominate British Rugby League at least until the era of Super League began in 1996.

On Saturday, January 7th 1989, Widnes were to contest the John Player Trophy Final against Wigan. The game was played at Burnden Park, Bolton before a crowd of 20,789. The debut of Jonathan Davies was therefore put on hold for a week and he did not play. One player who did play was Kurt Sorensen, who had only played in one of the last four games. And in the one he started at Warrington on Boxing Day, he had come off because a niggling injury. The Hulme brothers also played after being doubtful because of injury. The ultra-tough Paul Hulme was named as substitute forward. The Widnes team that faced Wigan in the 1989 John Player Trophy Final was:

Alan Tait, Rick Thackray, Andy Currier, Darren Wright, Martin Offiah, Tony Myler, David Hulme, Kurt Sorensen, Phil McKenzie, Joe Grima, Mike O'Neill, Emosi Koloto, Richie Eyres. Substitutes: Barry Dowd and Paul Hulme.

Unfortunately, Kurt Sorensen lost possession in the Widnes 25 in the opening minutes, and a slick Wigan move resulted in a unconverted try for their Kiwi centre Kevin Iro. The pitch was heavy after 24 hours of rain, and Wigan seemed to adapt to the conditions better. Against the run-of-play, Darren Wright quite literally snatched an equalising try for the Chemics. mid-way through the first-half. He intercepted a lofted pass by Wigan forward Adrian Shelford just inside his own half and raced 60 yards to score. Co-centre Andy Currier converted and suddenly Widnes were 6-4 in front. The Chemics hardly threatened again, but were still level at 6-6 with 10 minutes left. If their brilliant attack had got stuck on the heavy pitch, their resolute defence kept them in the game. That was until the great Ellery Hanley spotted half a gap as his team pressed the Widnes line again and scored the clinching converted try.

Jonathan comes North

Despite the narrowness of the defeat, the headline of Dave Candler's match-report was **"WOEFUL WIDNES!"**. I think the headline was harsh, it just wasn't the Chemics day, and they gave their all despite going down. Perhaps expectations were becoming very high of this exciting Widnes team. In his weekly column Doug Laughton implied as much and also expressed his disappointment at his team's performance. He wrote:

"The Rugby League game can be one of mixed emotions where anything can happen and the feeling one has in defeat can be different. There have been those in the past, such as the John Player semi-final against Warrington in 1986, when after defeat I was dismayed and I remember thinking that this could happen every time we play them.

I got the same uncomfortable feeling after the league games at Wigan and St Helens last season. However, after Saturday's defeat by Wigan in the final of the John Player, I was annoyed. Admittingly, Wigan are a top side but then so are we. On the day, however, we didn't do many things right."

Eight days after the loss to Wigan, the Chemics were to play Salford at home in their next league fixture. Jonathan Davies was one of the Widnes substitutes, and there was an 11,843 attendance for his debut. The Chemics put on another high-scoring show to win by 50 points to 8. The emphatic victory was marred by Tony Myler sustaining a broken ankle as his injury curse struck again. It was wretched and untimely luck for Myler. He had been having a great season and was back in the Great Britain side. There was even a picture of him in the match-programme along with Martin Offiah, David Hulme and Richie Eyres, who had also been selected for the forthcoming international against France. Tony had to leave the field just after half-time. In the first-half he'd scored a terrific try after selling several outrageous dummies using Martin Offiah as a foil. He also set up one of Martin's four tries.

In the 52nd minute of the game Jonathan Davies substituted Rick Thackray who had scored one of the Widnes tries. With his first touch of the ball he showed his startling speed off the mark, and left two Salford defenders in his wake before being tackled. He also showed some sound defence in an impressive debut. The headlines of Dave Candler's match-report alluded to Myler's injury, rather than the convincing Widnes win or the debut of Davies. It read **"CRUEL TWIST OF FATE"** with a sub-headline of "Ankle agony for Myler". Doug Laughton in his column also emphasised Tony's injury more than all else. Headlined: **"WE'LL MISS MYLER MAGIC"** it began:

"The injury to Tony Myler really ruined my day on Sunday. Not only will the side miss his silky skills and commitment, he's a great person to have around the club, and the way he's persevered in the face of adversity makes one proud to know him."

A fortnight later on January 29th, the Chemics faced Salford again away in the first round of the Challenge Cup. There was no 50-point romp this time, as Widnes rode their luck to progress to the second round by a narrow 18-14 margin. A couple of Salford errors resulted in two Widnes tries. Salford coach Kevin Ashcroft intimated after the game that his team had beaten themselves. Back in league action at Naughton Park on February 5th, the Chemics dispatched of relegation-haunted Oldham by 38 points to 14. Jonathan Davies who had been a substitute in the two encounters with Salford, played his first full game. He again impressed, scoring a try and kicking five goals. However, it was another player making his debut who stole the show. Eighteen-years old David Myers playing on the left-wing instead of Martin Offiah who was on international duty, scored a hat-trick. Rather like Keith Bentley, Myers was a very talented young local player who Doug sold. The circumstances of the Myers sale were different in that there was such a brilliant three-quarter line, a regular place was hard to come by.

Neither Davies or Myers were in the starting line-up for the second round of the Challenge Cup the following Saturday. Widnes had been drawn away to league leaders Castleford. Doug Laughton again named Jonathan as one of the substitutes, and in a seemingly tactical switch, the Hulme brothers filled the half-back positions. If it seemed a more defensive line-up, the first 25 minutes of the game shattered that illusion. Widnes scored four tries and were 22-0 ahead. It was the mobility of the forwards that produced the opening whirlwind. A forceful run by Richie Eyres and an offload to Alan Tait, linking up from the full-back position, sent the Flying Scotsman in for the opening try. Further tries from McKenzie, Grima and Koloto soon followed. Castleford scored a converted try before half-time and a further three penalty goals after the interval to get back in the game. They came within inches of another try, but Widnes - and specifically Emosi Koloto - had the final say. In a rare second-half Widnes attack, he prised an opening for Offiah to score. 'The Moose' then intercepted a Castleford passing movement to romp in from 25 yards to seal a 32-18 victory.

Before the third round, Widnes were to play Featherstone Rovers away on February 19th. Martin Offiah's try at Castleford was the 99th of his Rugby League career. He didn't waste time reaching his century at Featherstone. In the first minute of the game, he again raced 50 yards to reach the landmark. David Hulme also scored his 100th try for the Club in his 213th appearance. For good measure Offiah added another one five minutes from the end, taking a reverse pass from Mike O'Neill and speeding in from 20 yards. The Chemics 22-10 victory kept them well in the title hunt.

WEEKLY NEWS, THURSDAY, FEBRUARY 16, 1989 (Gp 8) 47

SPORT

―――― **Tongan giant keeps Widnes on Wembley trail** ――――

KOLOTO BLASTS BACK!

A FIERCE dressing down from Duggie Laughton spurred Emosi Koloto onto his sensational Man of the Match display on Saturday.

I can reveal that the Widnes coach fired his massive forward up with a behind-closed-doors, verbal attack in which he accused Koloto of a lack of aggression in recent Widnes games.

And the blasting from the normally taciturn Laughton certainly did the trick as Koloto delivered a fiery performance capped by two super tries that guided the Chemics comfortably into the quarter-finals of the Silk Cut Challenge Cup.

Laughton was quick to reward the mighty second rower with high praise, describing his display as the best from him since he flew to New Zealand to snap the star up last October.

David Candler at

CASTLEFORD 18PTS
WIDNES 32PTS

Wheldon Road

Grima was rewarded with a try himself after fine work by captain David Hulme, who gave a great leading show in the absence of injured Kurt Sorensen.

Widnes could have been further ahead but for Martin Offiah being obstructed as he roared towards the line on the left. Andy Currier, who missed the resultant penalty attempt, struggled to make his goal attempts count in a strong wind but

End of an Era

In the third round of the Challenge Cup, Widnes were drawn away to Leeds for another top-of-the-table confrontation. The headline of the preview of the game by Paul Cook in the *WWN* was " **It could be the game of the season.**" The preview began:

"While the BBC cameras will be at the Watersheddings for Oldham v Wigan, there's no doubt that the tie of the Silk Cut Challenge Cup quarter-finals is taking place at Headingley. Both sides were this week gearing up for what should be a titanic clash and one that the fans have shown they are desperate to see.

A Headingley spokesman said a crowd of 25,000 was to 30,000 expected for the tie. Widnes trained on Tuesday night with all - including skipper Kurt Sorensen - reporting a clean bill of health. Sorensen's inactivity in recent weeks however, could see the influential front-rower start the match on the bench."

The crowd prediction was accurate, the attendance was 26,100. Paul Cook's speculation that Kurt Sorensen would be one of the Widnes substitutes was also correct. What proved to be inaccurate was the headline, which implied it would be an evenly-matched contest. It was in fact no contest, as Doug Laughton's team turned on another top-notch performance to win by 24 points to 4. Widnes scored five tries with Joe Grima scoring two, David Hulme, Andy Currier and Martin Offiah - whose effort was a 75-yard interception - sharing the other three. Martin uncharacteristically, was one who spurned other chances to make the scoreline even more emphatic. He also made another spectacular 70-yard run earlier in the game, only to be surprisingly caught by Leeds international winger Phil Ford, who came across from the opposite wing to catch him. I'm pretty certain all of the travelling away fans were thrilled with the victory. Even so, the *WWN* report began:

"It's incredible to think that a 20-point defeat of Leeds at Headingley could be anything other than completely satisfying. Yet Widnes played such devastating rugby to storm into the Silk Cut Challenge Cup semi-finals that the winning margin barely describes their superiority. Now just one match remains between the Chemics and a richly deserved trip to Wembley, and from the way they played on Sunday, no-one will want to try and stop them.

The score line suggests a comfortable enough win, but it should have been so much more. The attacking play of Widnes was of the highest order - until they came to finish it off. The number of chances that went begging must have run close to double figures by the end of the match with Martin Offiah and Alan Tait missing the simplest. Widnes should have been out of sight by half-time such was the quality of their play."

Widnes were to face St Helens in the semi-final on March 11th again at Wigan's Central Park ground. In his *WWN* column Doug Laughton stated he was not taking anything for granted. Doug highlighted that the Saints had took his team all the way in the John Player semi-final. And it was St Helens who came out all guns blazing. An unconverted try by their left-winger Les Quirk gave the Saints a deserved lead. The Chemics, quickly delivered a reply when Joe Grima bust open the Saints defence on the half-way line, passed inside to Darren Wright who streaked away to the posts. Then after 20 minutes, came an incident which may have cost Widnes the game. Richie Eyres was controversially sent-off for tripping Saints stand-off half Neil Holding. Eyres did not trip Holding from behind, he was in front of him. It seemed to many – including BBC co-commentator Peter Fox –

more of a slip than a trip. Widnes were 8-12 down at half-time with Saints scrum-half Darren Bloor scoring under the posts just before the interval.

A man short and with St Helens playing out of their skins, the prospects of a Widnes victory looked unlikely. But as shown in previous games, Doug Laughton's side were not just about speed and flair, they had grit and resolve. Early in the second-half, the mighty Emosi Koloto created a gap for David Hulme to score a converted try which gave Widnes a 14-12 lead. Could the Chemics get another try to kill St Helens off? With eight minutes remaining, they nearly did. St Helens were in possession 25 yards from the Widnes try-line, when Neil Holding cross-kicked the ball to his left-wing. Andy Currier plucked the ball out of the air and sent Rick Thackray speeding down his wing. Rick raced 50 yards and seemed to have cleared a despairing ankle tap by Saints hooker Paul Groves. A split-second later he stumbled and the chance was gone. With three minutes left, the Saints took a rare second-half chance to score. Forty yards from the Widnes line, Groves found a gap in the Widnes defence, fed his left-centre Paul O'Loughlin, who passed to Les Quirk to score his second try of the game in the corner.

The 12 men of Widnes had got so close but were beaten by 16 points to 14. A bad refereeing decision had again contributed to Widnes going out of the Challenge Cup. Even an editorial in the *WWN* commented on the Eyres sending-off and the disallowed tries in the third round at Wigan the previous year. The editorial was headlined **"What must Widnes do to reach Wembley?"** Doug Laughton and his players now simply had to retain the Championship. After the anguish of the Challenge Cup semi-final defeat, Doug had stated that his team not winning anything was "unthinkable".

They had five league fixtures in March and apart from a draw at Bradford on March 19th, they won them all in convincing and Championship style. Warrington were thrashed 38-4 at Naughton Park on the Wednesday evening between the St Helens and Bradford games.

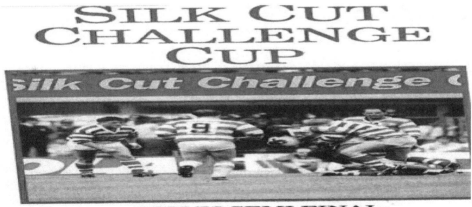

SILK CUT
CHALLENGE
CUP

1988/89 SEMI-FINAL
ST. HELENS v WIDNES
CENTRAL PARK, WIGAN
MARCH 11th 1989 3.00pm
PRICE 80p

Martin Offiah scored five of the six Widnes tries against Warrington. In doing so, like Andy Currier had done earlier in the season, he equalled the Club record for tries by a Widnes player in a game. A 35-6 thrashing was given to Oldham on their home ground the following Wednesday. This was the game when Jonathan Davies really arrived. Playing at stand-off half for only the second time, he scored two tremendous tries. The most satisfying in this series of high-scoring victories, was the 44-16 hammering of St Helens at Knowsley Road on Easter Monday. The most significant however, was the 36-4 defeat of Castleford at Naughton Park, three nights after gaining revenge for the Challenge Cup exit. The Chemics virtually knocked them out of the Championship race as they went to the top of the table themselves during the month.

Doug Laughton's team threatened to knock themselves out of the race for the Championship in the first two games in April. On April 2nd at Naughton Park, Bradford Northern went one better than the draw they earned in March at home to the Chemics. Harry Pinner exchanged to Leigh for Derek Pyke 14 months earlier, returned to haunt Widnes. After surging into an early 12-2 lead through converted tries by Andy Currier and Mike O'Neill, Pinner showed all his skills to lead Bradford to a 22-12 victory. Another 16-23 defeat was incurred away at Hull the following Wednesday night. Widnes were back on Humberside to face Hull Kingston Rovers on the Sunday. For an hour their Championship hopes hung by a thread as they trailed 6-13 with just 15 minutes left. A quick two-try burst by Emosi Koloto and Alan Tait gave them a slender 16-13 victory. Another narrow 24-22 victory came at Castleford on the next Wednesday. As in the Challenge Cup game in February, Koloto again scored two tries. It was Castleford's ninth league game without a win after being unbeaten and topping Division One until January.

Widnes were to play Wigan in their final league game of the season at Naughton Park on Sunday April 16th. It was literally a Championship decider, with the table-topping Chemics having accumulated 39 points from 25 games and second-placed Wigan 38 points from their 25. In contrast to Castleford, whose Championship challenge had collapsed, Wigan after losing five of their first nine league games, had lost only two of their next 16. They had also won the John Player Trophy and had again reached the Challenge Cup Final. They had reeled off 16 successive victories, 12 in the league and four in the Challenge Cup. Since their own Championship surge of 10 unbeaten games prior to April, Widnes seemed to be running out of gas. Two defeats and two narrow wins in the previous four games, did not bode well for the showdown even with home advantage. The form-book seemed to favour the Central Park team. They were though going have to win over Kurt Sorensen's dead body. Tucked next to the match-report of the Castleford game in the April 13th edition of the *WWN* was a headline that read: **" Captain Kurt: 'We will win' "** The article began:

"Widnes skipper Kurt Sorensen believes Sunday's title decider will be incentive enough to lift his side to one last mighty effort. With Wigan keeping their Championship challenge alive after a 14-7 win against St Helens last night, it all comes down to Sunday's game at Naughton Park. Speaking after last night's match, the Kiwi was well satisfied with the result. "On Sunday I think the whole occasion should inspire the players once again."

It certainly was an occasion, probably the momentous ever at the old Naughton Park ground. A crowd of 17,363 packed the terraces for this title-decider. It was the day after the tragic Hillsborough disaster, and there was a minute's silence for those who died at Hillsborough before the kick-off.

The Chemics made a disastrous start as Andy Currier's kick-off went on the full into touch. From the resulting penalty, Joe Lydon kicked Wigan to within 15 yards of the Widnes try-line. From only the second play-the-ball, forward Andy Platt went from acting half-back, and caught the Chemics defence cold to score a converted try. Also, early in the game David Hulme playing at stand-off, left the field injured. The Chemics replied when Eyres, Sorensen and substitute Barry Dowd combined to keep the ball alive. Dowd fed full-back Alan Tait who passed to Offiah who made short work of two Wigan defenders to score. Wigan scored another converted try, and were 12-4 ahead approaching the interval. Just on half-time, Offiah scored again following some superb handling. Dowd, Eyres and Tait were again involved. The final pass saw the quick-thinking Koloto parry the ball onto Mike O'Neill who surged forward into the Wigan 25. The ball was knocked from O'Neill's hands by a Wigan defender, Darren Wright hacked on and the ever-alert Offiah scooped the ball off the turf and raced over for a converted try.

In the first 15 minutes of the second-half Widnes put one hand on the Championship trophy. After just two minutes, Alan Tait raced 50 yards to take his team inside the Wigan 25. Within the set of six tackles, Kurt Sorensen barged over for a converted try and his side now led 16-12. Another try was needed and cometh the hour, cometh Martin Offiah. Five minutes later, Martin took a pass from Joe Grima inside his own half, he swerved inside one defender, raced between two more, left several more in futile pursuit, arced around Wigan full-back Steve Hampson to score a sensational try in the corner.

Martin Offiah on his way to his greatest and most important try for Widnes. Wigan were beaten 32-18 in the Championship "decider" at Naughton Park on April 16th 1989 - the day following the tragic Hillsborough disaster.

It was the most sensational of the many tries he scored for Widnes and also the timeliest. Minutes later Widnes again come from near their own 25 into the Wigan 25 via a great break by Koloto and carried on by Grima. Again, before a set of six was complete, Paul Hulme playing at scrum-half had plunged over for another try. Soon after Koloto was sent-off for a high-tackle. Ellery Hanley scored a converted try for Wigan but the 12 men of Widnes not only hung on, Phil McKenzie scored another converted try in the last minute to seal a 32-18 triumph.

There were jubilant scenes at the end. As in the last league home league game of the 1987/88 season when the Championship was virtually clinched, Martin Offiah was chaired off the field after having scored a superb hat-trick. The man-of-the-match award though was given to Kurt Sorensen. This second Championship was in many ways more satisfying than the previous year. Doug Laughton's team had stuffed their main rivals in a straight shoot-out. Wigan's New Zealand coach Graham Lowe who dubbed this great Widnes team as "the nearly men" was made to eat his words. They had also scored 726 points against Wigan's 543 in their 26 league fixtures and conceded just 345 against Wigan's 434.

In the *WWN* Doug spoke confidently about winning a third successive Championship. He was again looking ahead, and had signed forward Paul Moriarty from Welsh Rugby Union at the end of March. Praising all the players who had contributed to the retaining of the Championship, he highlighted Mike O'Neill who was in his testimonial season. Doug intimated that Mike was playing better than ever. It was left now for his team to add the Premiership to their Championship. They duly reached the Premiership Final at Old Trafford by defeating Bradford Northern and then St Helens by 30-18 and 32-14 respectively at Naughton Park.

The two Premiership games saw the return to the side of right-winger Rick Thackray and forward Derek Pyke. Neither had played during the Championship run-in. Thackray scored one try against Bradford and two against St Helens. Even so he was not picked for the final and Pyke was only a substitute. Doug Laughton was easing Jonathan Davies into Rugby League by playing him on the right-wing. Davies was also gradually taking over goal-kicking duties from Andy Currier. Another player back in the team as substitute against St Helens after his injury was Tony Myler. Coming on in the second-half he played a part in three second-half tries including one of Thackray's. Whilst Thackray helped himself to three tries over the Premiership games, the unstoppable Martin Offiah scored five. His hat-trick against Bradford was his eighth of the season. The Champions were to face fourth-placed Hull in the 1989 Premiership Final at Old Trafford on May 14th. The team was:

Alan Tait, Jonathan Davies, Andy Currier, Darren Wright, Martin Offiah, David Hulme, Paul Hulme, Kurt Sorenson, Phil McKenzie, Joe Grima, Mike O'Neill, Emosi Koloto, Richie Eyres, Substitutes: **Tony Myler and Derek Pyke.**

After 12 minutes play, the Chemics went ahead when Emosi Koloto sent Darren Wright streaking 40 yards for a converted try. Hull however, were proving a tough nut to crack. The Humberside team's inspirational Welsh half-back Gary Pearce scored a converted try to level the scores. Approaching half-time Hull were leading 8-6, when a sensational try by Andy Currier put Widnes back in front. As in the Challenge Cup semi-final he plucked a kick by the opposition out the air. This time from a full 90 yards, he raced straight down the right-wing to score. Two minutes into the second-half Martin Offiah as he often did, popped up from nowhere away from his left-wing spot to race 30 yards for the third Widnes try. It was his 58th of the season and his 100th for the Club. It seemed there was to be another avalanche of Widnes tries. Martin's try was in fact the last of the game, as a determined Hull side held the Chemics to a 10-18 losing margin. Widnes were the first club to win both the Championship and Premiership Trophy in successive seasons.

On May 27th the Chemics were to compete in France for the European Trophy against St Esteve. It was a play-off to decide who would contest the World Club Championship the following season. Two coaches of Widnes fans missed the game because of traffic congestion. The Chemics did not have to "compete" at all, as they inflicted a 60-6 massacre. This was achieved without Alan Tait, Andy Currier and Martin Offiah. Tait was injured, whilst Currier and Offiah had flown to Australia to play club football there. Back on the right-wing was Rick Thackray who scored four of the 12 Widnes tries. It was "slick Rick's" swansong. His modest try-scoring record of 32 tries in 78 games for Widnes does not I think do justice to his talent. Perhaps during his time at Widnes, the ball had been going more to Offiah, or moves had been finished off by the side's other speed-merchants. It's a pity he could not get clear of an ankle tap in the Challenge Cup semi-final against St Helens. He really would have been part of Widnes RLFC folk-lore had he done so.

Prior to the game in France, in addition to predicting a third successive Championship in the 1989/90 season, Doug Laughton stated in the *WWN* that the Club was "set up for years to come." The team and the Club should have been set up for years to come. Jonathan Davies, David Hulme, and Phil McKenzie were only in their mid-20s. Alan Tait, Andy Currier, Darren Wright, Martin Offiah, Paul Hulme, Richie Eyres and Emosi Koloto were only in their early 20s. Only King Kurt Sorensen was over 30. In fact, Doug's team reached what I think was a pre-mature peak early in the 1989/90 season, when they achieved the most famous victory in the Club's history.

That victory however, was I believe a contributory factor in the Chemics not winning a third successive Championship. Although another controversial refereeing decision in a league game in January 1990 may have been a reason also.

It's make or break!

Championship trip turned into French farce 130 fans miss game

Fixtures, results, attendances and points scorers 1988/89 season

Opposition	Venue	Result	Attend.	Goals	Tries
AUGUST					
21 Wigan (Charity Shield).	Isle of Man	20-14	5,044	Currier (4)	McKenzie, Wright, Offiah
28 Halifax	Away	20-26	9,001	Currier (2)	McKenzie, Offiah, Wright, Dowd
SEPTEMBER					
4 Hull	Home	30- 8	5,435	Kebbie (5)	Offiah (4), M. O'Neill, Sorensen, Wright
11 Leeds	Away	30-14	12,498	Dowd (2), Currier	Thackray (3). Tait, Sorensen, McKenzie
18 St Helens (Lancashire Cup 1)	Home	32-24	10,764	Currier (4)	Offiah (2). Wright, Tait, Sorensen, Currier
25 Featherstone Rovers	Home	59- 2	5,195	Currier (7)	Currier (5). Offiah (4), D. Hulme, Tait
28 Swinton (Lancashire Cup 2)	Home	38- 4	4,988	Currier (5)	P. Hulme (2), T. Myler (2), D. Hulme, Tait, Offiah
OCTOBER					
2 Salford	Away	12-15	6,684	Currier (2)	Tait, Offiah
9 Halifax	Home	5- 4	6,971	Currier, S. O'Neill dg	Currier
12 Wigan (Lancashire Cup semi)	Away	10-14	17,813	Currier (3)	M. O'Neill
23 Wakefield Trinity	Away	28-14	5,069	Currier (4)	Wright (3), McKenzie, Thackray
NOVEMBER					
6 Wigan	Away	24-10	16,595	Currier (4)	Sorensen, Tait, Offiah, Wright
13 Featherstone Rovers (John Player 1)	Home	37-12	5,299	Currier (6), Tait dg	Offiah (3), T. Myler, Sorensen, D. Hulme
20 Hull Kingston Rovers	Home	43- 6	5,532	Currier (5), D.Hulme dg	Sorensen (2), Offiah (2), T. Myler (2), Tait, Grima
27 Sheffield Eagles (John Player 2)	Away	32- 9	2,716	Currier (6)	Thackray, Offiah, Tait T. Myler, Koloto
DECEMBER					
3 Warrington (John Player 3)	Home	16 - 7	6,449	Currier (2)	Offiah (2), McKenzie
10 St Helens (John Player semi)	Wigan	20-18	6,755	Currier (2)	Offiah (2), Currier, Eyres
14 Wakefled Trinity	Home	40-12	4,960	Currier (4)	Currier (2), T. Myler, Tait, Offiah, Kebbie, D. Hulme, Koloto
18 Leeds	Home	8-20	7,396	Currier (2)	Offiah
26 Warrington	Away	18- 8	6,219	Currier (3)	M. O'Neill, Wright, Thackray
JANUARY					
1 St Helens	Home	29-22	11,875	Currier (4), dg	Tait, T. Myler, D. Hulme, Wright, Offiah
7 Wigan (John Player Final).	Bolton	6-12	20,709	Currier	Wright
15 Salford	Home	50-12	11,871	Currier (7)	Offiah (4), Grima, M. O'Neill T. Myler, Thackray, Tait
29 Salford (Challenge Cup 1).	Away	18-14	7,094	Currier	M. O'Neill, D. Hulme, Offiah, Tait
FEBRUARY					
5 Oldham	Home	38-14	9,264	Davies (5)	Myers (3), D. Hulme, McKenzie, M. O'Neill, Davies,
11 Castleford (Challenge Cup 2)	Away	32-18	19,765	Currier (4)	Koloto (2), Tait, McKenzie, Grima, Offiah
19 Featherstone Rovers	Away	22-10	6,132	Currier	Offiah (2), D. Hulme, Thackray, M. O'Neill
26 Leeds (Challenge Cup 3)	Away	24- 4	26,303	Currier (2)	Grima (2), Currier, Offiah, Eyres
MARCH					
11 St Helens (Challenge Cup semi)	Away	14-16	17,119	Currier (3)	Wright, D. Hulme
15 Warrington	Home	32- 4	8,947	Currier (4)	Offiah (5), Tait
19 Bradford Northern	Away	16-16	5,332	Currier (2)	Wright (2), Currier
22 Oldham	Away	35-16	6,776	Davies (5) dg	Davies (2), Wright (2), Offiah, Thackray
27 St Helens	Away	44-16	16,009	Davies (8)	Offiah (3), D. Hulme, Currier, Eyres, Davies
30 Castleford	Home	36- 4	11,024	Davies (6)	D. Hulme (3), Offiah (2), Currier
APRIL					
2 Bradford Northern	Home	12-22	9,537	Currier (2)	Currier, M. O'Neill
6 Hull	Away	16-23	7,236	Davies (4)	Davies, Tait
9 Hull Kingston Rovers	Away	16-13	7,844	Davies (2)	Currier, Koloto, Tait
12 Castleford	Away	24-22	6,364	Currier (4)	Koloto (2), Currier, Offiah
16 Wigan	Home	32-18	17,323	Davies (4)	Offiah (3), Sorensen, P. Hulme, McKenzie
23 Bradford Northern (Premiership 1)	Home	30-18	8,483	Currier (5)	Offiah (3), Thackray, McKenzie
MAY					
7 St Helens (Premiership 2)	Home	38-14	12,484	Davies (5)	Offiah (2), Thackray (2), Wright, M. O'Neill, Eyres
14 Hull (Premiership Final	Manchester	18-10	40,194	Davies (3	Wright, Currier, Offiah
27 St Esteve (European Cup)	Away	60- 6		Davies (5), Kebbie (3)	Thackray (4), Davies (2), Kebbie, Grima (2), Marsh, Moriarty

Players total number of games and points 1988/89 season

	Played	Goals	Tries	Points
Chris Ashurst	1			
Andy Currier	41	(1dg) 106	18	285
Jonathan Davies	16	(1dg) 47	7	123
Barry Dowd	25	2	1	8
Andy Eyres	1			0
Richie Eyres	41		4	16
Joe Grima	38		7	28
David Hulme	39	(1dg)	13	53
Paul Hulme	39		3	12
Brimah Kebbie	3	8	2	24
Emosi Koloto	30		7	28
David Marsh	8		1	4
Phil McKenzie	41		9	36
Paul Moriarty	5		1	4
David Myers	8		3	12
John Myler	1			0
Tony Myler	23		9	36
Keith Newton	1			0
Mike O'Neill	42		9	36
Steve O.Neill	4	(1dg)		1
Martin Offiah	41		58	232
Duncan Platt	2			0
Derek Pyke	31			0
David Smith	3			0
Kurt Sorensen	30		8	32
Alan Tait	39	(1dg)	16	65
Rick Thackray	31		16	64
Darren Wright	38		18	72

First Division	Games	Won	Drawn	Lost	For	Against	Points
Widnes	26	20	1	5	726	345	41
Wigan	26	19	0	7	535	434	38
Leeds	26	18	0	8	530	380	36
Hull	26	17	0	9	427	355	34
Castleford	26	15	2	9	601	480	32
Featherstone Rovers	26	13	1	12	482	545	27
St Helens	26	12	1	13	513	529	25
Bradford Northern	26	11	1	14	545	518	23
Wakefield Trinity	26	11	1	14	413	540	23
Salford	26	11	0	15	469	526	22
Warrington	26	10	0	16	456	455	20
Oldham	26	8	1	17	462	632	17
Halifax	26	6	1	19	335	535	13
Hull Kingston Rovers	26	6	1	19	408	636	13

4) 1989/90 season "World Club Champions"

British Rugby League was vibrant in the late 1980s and early 1990s. Attendances had been generally rising at games throughout the 1980s. In the 1988/89 season average attendances for league games at Naughton Park had risen to 8,648. Wigan had the highest average league attendances with 14,543. Leeds and St Helens also had better gates than Widnes, averaging 12,060 and 9,514 respectively. Playing standards also seemed to be rising. The 1988 Great Britain tourists had beaten Australia in a Test match for the first time in a decade. In the next series in England in 1990, Great Britain defeated them again and came within whisker of a second victory and re-gaining the Ashes. Martin Offiah and Wigan's Ellery Hanley were the biggest personalities in British RL for many a long year. Along with the signing of Jonathan Davies by Widnes, Offiah and Hanley enhanced the game's national profile.

Television coverage also I believe was enhanced in the 1980s when Ray French began commentating for the BBC. The best coverage of the game however in my opinion before or since, was by the ITV in this particular era when Clive Tyldesley - who was a soccer commentator on Radio City for many years - provided commentary. The ITV covered the Charity Shield game between the Champions Widnes and Challenge Cup holders Wigan on August 27th. It was a repeat of the previous year's encounter, but the venue this time was Anfield, the famous home of Liverpool FC. The Chemics had lost the previous week again to St Helens in a pre-season friendly, but this was the "friendly" that really mattered.

Just after the Chemics kicked off, Clive Tyldesley - in his debut RL commentary - said "We'll see from the early tackles whether this is a pre-season friendly or not". When Kurt Sorensen then immediately clattered a Wigan forward Tyldesley quickly added "the answer is "no". The game was indeed fiery and competitive, and it was Wigan who were ahead 16-7 at the interval. In the first 10 minutes of the second-half, the Chemics had turned the game around with three quick-fire tries. The catalyst of the come-back was Derek Pyke, a second=half substitute for Joe Grima. His deft handling skills helped set up tries for wingers Brimah Kebbie and Martin Offiah. In between those two efforts, Jonathan Davies had also scored one. Widnes eventually won the game 27 points to 22. The headline of Dave Candler's match-report accurately read "IT'S DEADLY DEREK'S KISS OF LIFE".

In his *WWN* column Doug Laughton expressed his satisfaction with the team's performance. Doug also suggested that Anfield should be the permanent venue for the Charity Shield. In the 1989/90 season Doug also wrote a column in the programmes for home games. In the programme for the first league home game against Salford on September 3rd, Doug wrote again of his satisfaction with the team's performance against Wigan. He highlighted the performance not only of Derek Pyke, but also the performances of Jonathan Davies and Kurt Sorensen. Widnes made another statement of intent for the new season by thrashing Salford 46-8. Right-winger Brimah Kebbie showed tremendous speed scoring one of eight Widnes tries. The headlines of the *WWN* match-report alluded to Kebbie's try reading **"WINGER MAKES PERFECT START TO THE SEASON."**

The headline could easily have described collectively all five of his games in September 1989. The four remaining games in the month were won as the whole team also made a perfect start. Two more league games at Hull on September 10th and at home to Featherstone Rovers on September 24th were won 26-11 and 59-8 respectively. The Hull game was quite literally hard-fought. A brawl involving all players broke out after Hull forward Andy Dannatt poleaxed Alan Tait and Kurt Sorensen attacked Dannatt. Kurt was sin-binned, and in the second-half sent-off in a separate incident. The Chemics also progressed to the Lancashire Cup semi-finals with a 46-6 first round victory at Carlisle on September 17th and a 34-12 second round victory at Leigh on September 27th.

Brimah Kebbie scored in the first three of the four games, scoring four tries in the successive games against Carlisle and Featherstone Rovers. Martin Offiah also scored four tries against Featherstone as he did in the 1988/89 fixture. Even Martin though had never scored four tries in successive games as Kebbie had done. Up until the Lancashire Cup game at Leigh, Kebbie was leading try-scorer having scored 11 to Offiah's 10. Almost inevitably, Martin edged ahead by scoring two more at Leigh, whilst Brimah drew his first blank of the season. Even so, "Little Martin" was becoming a favourite with Widnes fans. Indeed, the headline for the report of the Carlisle game in the *WWN* read: **"KEBBIE SCORES WITH THE FANS"**. The downside of the Carlisle game was that Emosi Koloto incurred a long-term neck injury.

THE WIDNES TEAM AFTER WINNING THE 1989 CHARITY SHIELD AT ANFIELD.
BACK LEFT TO RIGHT: Alan Tait, Emosi Koloto, Joe Grima, Mike O'Neill, Paul Hulme, Derek Pyke, Tony Myler.
David Marsh, David Hulme. FRONT: Brimah Kebbie, Kurt Sorensen, Darren Wright, Richie Eyres, Martin Offiah.

Playing his first game of the season at Leigh was Andy Currier. He had just returned from Australia, where he had been sensation during the summer playing for Balmain. He had arrived belatedly as Balmain had reached the Australian Grand Final. His return was quite timely, as Widnes were to face Canberra Raiders for the World Club Championship at Old Trafford on the night of October 4th. Andy was optimistic about his team's chances of winning. In the September 28th edition of the *WWN* he was quoted as saying:

"I'm confident Widnes can beat Canberra next week. We've got a great side and I'm looking forward to renewing my acquaintance with Laurie Daley who I was up against last Sunday."

In contrast, Doug Laughton stated in his book *A Dream Come True* that after watching a Canberra training session he feared a beating - although he did not reveal his thoughts to his players. Doug perhaps surprisingly, relegated free-scoring Brimah Kebbie to being one of four substitutes to accommodate Andy Currier on the right-wing. Jonathan Davies was selected to play in Currier's usual right-centre position. The full Widnes line-up was:

Alan Tait, Andy Currier, Jonathan Davies, Darren Wright, Martin Offiah, Tony Myler, David Hulme, Joe Grima, Phil McKenzie, Derek Pyke, Kurt Sorensen, Paul Hulme, Richie Eyres. Substitutes: Brimah Kebbie, Barry Dowd, Mike O'Neill and David Smith.

The official attendance for the game which was televised by the BBC was 30,786. For most of the first-half, the Raiders showed just why the Australians had been dominating international Rugby League for the previous two decades. Doug Laughton's pessimism seemed to be justified as his team was hit by a whirlwind. Canberra's team of Australian internationals scored 12 points in the first 12 minutes, displaying pace, power, brilliant handling and teamwork. They had another try disallowed, and could have been out of sight in the first half-hour. Alex Murphy co-commentating for the BBC was not exaggerating when he stated in the first-half "had this been a boxing match it would have been stopped".

The Chemics somehow come off the canvas, and reduced the deficit to two points by the interval. In the 27th minute for the first time they got within 25 yards of the Canberra try-line. Joe Grima made a half-break, passed to David Hulme who in turn passed to brother Paul, who plunged over for a converted try. Five minutes later, a typical deft pass by Derek Pyke made an opening for Phil McKenzie, who sent Martin Offiah in for another try. Martin's effort was not converted, but Widnes were right back in the game trailing only 10-12 at the interval. The influential seasoned Australian international Mel Meninga, who had scored the first, and had a hand in the second Canberra try, did not come out for the second-half. Widnes also lost Tony Myler early in the half because of a head gash.

Within 10 minutes of the re-start the Chemics had turned the game completely around, scoring two unconverted and one converted try. First, Jonathan Davies despite being nearly decapitated by opposing centre Laurie Daley, squeezed in at the right-hand corner to give his team the lead. Daley was sin-binned and fortunate not to be sent-off. Two minutes later Joe Grima made another break from just outside his own 25. He handed on to Darren Wright, who in turn passed to

Martin Offiah who sped in for his second try. Martin then turned try-provider, when he sent Richie Eyres in for a try which was converted. The Raiders were suddenly 12-24 down but almost got back into the game in the last 10 minutes. Laurie Daley back on the field, looked to have scored a try but the lost ball when grounding. Kurt Sorensen took a quick tap on his team's 25, fed substitute Barry Dowd who sold two dummies in a 45-yard run. Barry passed to the supporting Darren Wright, who went under the posts to seal the victory. Canberra did subsequently score another converted try to make the final score Widnes 30 Canberra Raiders 18. `

Doug Laughton's team were World Club Champions. Who could stop them? they seemed invincible. The answer was provided within a week, as they slumped to a 6-31 defeat at Sheffield and were dumped out of the Lancahsire Cup at Warrington, again just scoring just 6 points as the Wires scored 28. Doug's latest signing from Rugby Union Welsh centre John Devereux, made his debut in this game coming as a substitute. In the *WORLD CHAMPIONS '89* booklet which was published to commemorate the 25th anniversary of the WWC victory, Kurt Sorensen is quoted as saying:

"It dazzled us for a few weeks afterwards - we weren't at our best as we were still on a massive high. We'd walk around town feeling ten foot high as we were buzzing that much. We had our head in the clouds and the best example of that was the week after the WCC we go to Sheffield and get well beat."

The players seemed to have their heads in the clouds for longer than a few weeks to me. There were some great performances in the 1989/90 season, but there were also several indifferent ones that I think may have cost a third successive Championship, and possibly a place in the 1990 Challenge Cup Final. The World Club Championship victory was a great achievement and occasion. I personally though would have traded it for another Championship, or winning the Challenge Cup at Wembley. The fact that neither was achieved I think had ramifications.

Widnes captain Kurt Sorensen lifts the World Club Championship Trophy after the defeat of Canberra Raiders on the night of October 4th 1989 at Old Trafford. Martin Offiah, Paul Hulme and Richie Eyres raise arms in triumph.

End of an Era

The Word Club Champions got back to winning ways with a 30-10 home victory over Wakefield and a 28-16 away victory at Salford. The Wakefield victory was uninspiring despite a fine performance by Tony Myler and a Martin Offiah hat-trick. More concerning than the performance, was the jeering of Andy Currier when he scored a second-half try. It seems some supporters were angered by an apparent transfer request by Currier. Brimah Kebbie was cheered when he came as substitute. In the October 19th edition of the *WWN* Doug Laughton stated his fury at the jeers directed at Andy. There were also two letters from supporters who thought the barracking was in bad taste, Brimah Kebbie was back in the starting line-up at Salford and was amongst the try-scorers. Andy Currier perhaps silenced some of his detractors at Salford by scoring two more tries. The match-report in the *WWN* began:

"Transfer seeking Andy Currier forgot his off-field troubles and showed his class with two well taken tries. The Great Britain centre who had a transfer request turned down twice by Widnes last week but has failed to show the sparkling form which made him a hero in Australia over the summer."

Currier had played for Great Britain in the first Test against the New Zealand tourists at Old Trafford in the week between the games against Wakefield and Salford. Also selected for Great Britain were Alan Tait, Martin Offiah and David Hulme. Kurt Sorensen was selected for New Zealand who won the Test 24-16 The highlight of the match was a sensational Martin Offiah try. A summarised report of the game was in the October 26th edition of the *WWN*. I found it interesting to read that the report described the 18,273 attendance for the 1989 Old Trafford Test match as "disappointing". New Zealand touring teams were never traditionally the attraction the Australians were. When one considers that the highest attendance of the three Tests between GB and the Kiwis in 1980 was 10.948, the attendance at Old Trafford in 1989 was an indication of how the state of British Rugby League had improved. An 18,000- plus attendance at the start of the decade would have been anything but disappointing.

In the November 2nd edition of the *WWN* it was stated that attendances at club games had also been disappointing. It was also written that a 10,000 gate was expected at Naughton Park when the tourists played Widnes three days later. As it transpired, 9,905 spectators saw New Zealand defeat the Chemics 26-18. The tourist's management must have rated Kurt Sorensen highly, as he was not in the touring party. Despite playing for his country in the the Test series, Kurt played for Widnes against his fellow countrymen in between the Tests! In fact, he helped set up the first Widnes try against the Kiwis by sending Brimah Kebbie flying down the wing. Kebbie passed on to Alan Tait who completed a spectacular 80-yard move.

Despite winning the first Test, the New Zealand tourists lost the remaining two Tests and the series. Kurt Sorensen had played in all three encounters for the Kiwis, whilst Martin Offiah and David Hulme played for Great Britain in all three In addition, Alan Tait and Paul Hulme played in two of them and Andy Currier one. The week after Great Britain clinched the series, in his column headlined **"Test players we can all be proud of"** Doug Laughton wrote:

"The Widnes players in the test series certainly did us all proud. Martin Offiah proved beyond all reasonable doubt that he is now the complete wingman and winning the man-of-the match award. David and Paul Hulme were there usual determined, persistent and aggressive selves with Alan Tait looking quite majestic at full-back.

It is fair to say Widnes and its players have done a great deal for international Rugby League these past few months, starting with the defeat of Canberra Raiders and the subsequent fine performances of all players winning the test series on home soil for the first time in 24 years: Unfortunately, it has not much done much for us on the domestic scene. After the Canberra game we slumped to two successive defeats at Sheffield Eagles in the league and Warrington in the semi-final of the Lancashire Cup. "

Doug did not refer to the 16-14 home defeat lowly Leigh inflicted on his team the day after the third Test. Like the Sheffield game, it was one that might have been lost because of the Canberra effect. Another defeat at Leeds on November 19th left Widnes six points behind league leaders Wigan. Martin Offiah scored both Widnes tries in the 12-26 loss and was clobbered by a Leeds defender scoring his second. The incident epitomised a lot of the rough stuff that went on in the game. In the 15th minute Paul Moriarty in only his fifth first-team game for Widnes was sent-off. Perhaps still trying to make an impact in Rugby League, the former Welsh Rugby Union forward had such an impact on the jaw of Leeds forward Hugh Waddell he broke it. On the stroke of half-time there was a repeat of the scene at Hull when all players of both sides were involved in a mass brawl. The police had to help the referee to stop the fighting. The brawl made the front-page of the November 23rd edition of the *WWN* and the headline read: **"NO POLICE ACTION ON PUNCH UP."**

NO POLICE ACTION ON PUNCH-UP

POLICE will take no action over Sunday's mass brawl between Widnes and Leeds players which spilled over into the crowd.

It seems the referee took lenient action himself, as only Joe Grima and Leeds forward Craig Izzard were sin-binned. The following Saturday the Chemics got back to winning ways with a 24-16 home victory over Castleford before the ITV cameras. The channel's coverage of Rugby League since the start of the season and the commentary of Clive Tyldesley was praised in the match-programme. Some great Widnes tries were televised, particularly a superb side-stepping 50-yard effort by Jonathan Davies. His Welsh compatriot John Devereux also scored his first try for the Club. On the downside, Joe Grima was again sin-binned for pouncing on Castleford hooker Graham Southernwood when he was on the floor.

The Chemics first two games in December were away games in the Regal Trophy - the John Player Trophy had a new sponsor and therefore a new name for the 1989/90 season. In the first round against Second Division Nottingham, they progressed with an emphatic 48-18 victory. Wingmen Brimah Kebbie and Martin Offiah scored a hat-trick and a brace of tries respectively. The best Widnes try of the game however was again scored by Jonathan Davies from the full-back position. Late in the game, he took a Paul Hulme pass from virtually under the Widnes posts, and streaked downfield straight as an arrow to score under the Nottingham posts. The Welsh wizard's only diversion en route was to sidestep past Nottingham full-back Chris Williss.

The second round on December 7th was a completely different story and outcome. In a repeat of the previous season's final. the Widnes try-scoring machine was again completely stilted in another televised game at Central Park, Wigan. The Chemics great rivals seemed to be going from strength to strength under their new Australian coach John Monie. The 18-0 Wigan victory not only reflected the game, but perhaps also the current form of the two sides. It was to be Brimah Kebbie's last appearance for the Chemics. Despite averaging a try a game in his 16 first-team appearances, Doug Laughton it seems only ever regarded Kebbie as a "minor signing". The Wigan game it seemed for a short period to be Joe Grima's last game for the Club also. After being sin-binned at Leeds and home to Castleford, 'Smokin Joe' was sent-off at Wigan for a high tackle. In his December 20th *WWN* column Doug wrote:

"The decision to cross Joe Grima off the register was not taken lightly. It is fair to say that I had been having a few goes at Joe about his discipline of late. But having bought him at as a bargain buy from Swinton and the good service, he has given the club, this week's decision has left me sad."

Doug's December 20th column was written between two of his team's emphatic league victories over Barrow 34-4 away and 48-0 at Naughton Park. They did not necessarily indicate a return to vintage form, as Barrow were the Division One whipping boys in the 1989/90 season. They had been promoted from the Second Division the previous season, but found the First Division too hot to handle. They finished bottom of the division and were relegated, winning only one league game. Over the course of the two games, the Chemics scored an aggregate of 15 tries. Curiously, only one of them was scored by Martin Offiah. Almost inevitably, Martin scored three of the six Widnes tries in the next game at home against Warrington on Boxing Day. He always seemed to come back with a bang after any lulls in his relentless try-scoring. John Devereux on the right-wing also scored a couple, and it was he who got the headlines of the *WWN* match-report which read " **DEVEREUX MAKES MARK AT LAST**" the report began:

"John Devereux has arrived as a genuine Rugby League talent. Martin Offiah may have scored a marvellous hat-trick, but it was the former Welsh rugby union player who showed something that little bit extra in Boxing Day's vital derby win. Playing on the right-wing in place of transfer-seeking Brimah Kebbie, Devereux displayed tremendous speed and power to grab two storming tries."

Devereux or "Devs" as he came to be known to many Widnes fans, was indeed an accomplished player. Though perhaps not as fast as Kebbie whom he replaced, or Tait, Davies, Offiah, Currier and Wright, he was certainly no slouch. Devereux was also well-built and tremendously brave and strong both in attack and defence. As Brimah Kebbie had the shortest, John Devereux had the longest career at Widnes of all the signings from Rugby Union that Doug Laughton made. His time at Widnes stretched beyond the start of the Super League era until 1997. Kebbie was transfer-listed for £95,000 in January 1990.

The Chemics began the new decade with a fourth successive league victory at St Helens winning by 18 points to 8. The pitch was heavy and it was a dour and at times dull struggle, with the backs getting few running chances. Even so, any defeat of the Saints was satisfactory, and the latest two points had hauled Widnes back into the Championship race. One player who was not slowed down by the conditions was fleet-footed Jonathan Davies. Playing on the left-wing in place of the injured Martin Offiah, he converted two of the few passes he received into glorious tries. On a minor roll, Widnes were at home to Leeds on January 7th. In his testimonial season, Tony Myler also wrote a column in the match-programme. In the programme for the Leeds game he stated:

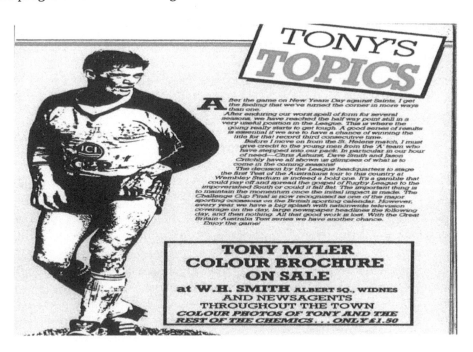

50

"After the game on New Year's Day against Saints, I get the feeling we've turned the corner in more ways than one. After enduring our worst spell of form, we have reached the half way point still in a very useful position in the League."

Tony either spoke or wrote too soon. The Chemics were again lack-lustre, as Leeds won at Naughton Park for the second successive season. Co-incidentally, the 20-8 scoreline was exactly the same as in the 1988/89 season. Curiously, the game also followed a similar pattern to the previous season's fixture, with Widnes taking an early lead before eventually losing. In the ninth minute Phil McKenzie kicked ahead only to be obstructed by Leeds full-back Garry Lord. It did not matter as Paul Hulme pounced on the rolling ball for a converted try. McKenzie was the only Widnes player in form, and was something of a lone ranger trying to turn the tide. Another 6-16 defeat at Bradford on the evening of January 17th, was a further blow in the quest for a third successive Championship. Paul Moriarty back after suspension for his sending off at Leeds, scored the only Widnes try. Joe Grima was also back in the side after suspension. The decision to cancel his contract was reversed.

The Chemics just managed to keep alive their receding hopes of retaining the Championship on the Saturday following the loss at Bradford. They defeated Castleford away in a hard-fought game televised by the ITV. Like the Leeds game, it took a similar pattern to the previous season's fixture which the Chemics won 24-22. It would have been again an identical scoreline but for Martin Offiah's fourth try in the final minute. It was destiny wasn't it? Martin had not scored in the defeats against Leeds and Bradford. The WWN report began:

"Martin Offiah rediscovered his Midas touch to launch his try scoring campaign for the decade in spectacular style. And the Chemics needed every one of his four tries as they battled ferociously against a spirited second half fight back by Castleford to claim their first win in three matches."

Exactly a fortnight after the victory at Castleford, the ITV cameras were at Naughton Park for the next league game at home to Wigan. Doug Laughton's team really needed to defeat their rivals and league leaders to stay in the Championship race. The omens were not that good. The previous week the Chemics had a difficult encounter at home to the first round of the Challenge Cup. They defeated Second Division Batley 26-10, but it was another example of their patchy form. The victory was marred by the sending-off of Andy Currier by referee John Holdsworth. He was the referee who controversially sent-off Richie Eyres in the previous season's semi-final. David Hulme was also stretchered off and unfit for the crucial Wigan game. Tony Myler, Paul Hulme, Derek Pyke and Richie Eyres were also injured and unavailable for the Wigan game. With Currier suspended despite an appeal against his sending off against Batley, six players who were in the victorious World Club Championship team game were not in the line-up against Wigan.

Doug Laughton re-shuffled the team for the game, selecting Phil McKenzie at scrum-half and giving a debut to Steve McCurrie at hooker. McCurrie still had not reached his 17th birthday. The clash did not provide much of the flowing rugby of the previous season's Championship "decider", yet was equally compelling and, on this occasion, controversial. In the 26th minute Widnes drew first blood after an incursion into the Wigan 25. Jonathan Davies hoisted a huge "bomb" which bamboozled Wigan full-back Ged Byrne. He failed to catch the ball, as Jonathan followed up to touch down his own kick, he was just beaten to the ball by David Marsh playing at right-centre in place of Andy Currier. Davies converted, but five minutes later Wigan were level when they made an attack in the opposite 25. A bad pass was thrown along the Wigan line and the ball went to ground. Ellery Hanley showed split-second quick-thinking and hacked the ball forward, chased after it and scored a converted try. By half-time the league leaders had forged ahead with a penalty goal by 17-year-old Widnes born scrum-half Bobby Goulding.

A drop-goal by Goulding early in the second-half stretched Wigan's lead to 9-6. In the last five minutes, the Chemics threw everything they had at the visitors. A match-winning try was needed if they were to stay in the Championship race. Tension was fever pitch as the Chemics forced a series of sets of six near the Wigan line. In the very last minute of normal time, Phil McKenzie made a sort of lateral run from dummy-half. Just before Phil made his run, Clive Tyldesley stated in his commentary "It's now or never for Widnes" and when McKenzie ran with the ball he commented "McKenzie! Grima! Sorensen! Offiah! can he get there! yes he can! Martin Offiah who else?" Who else indeed but Martin Offiah in his 100th game for the Club, could have snatched victory right at the end? It was not as spectacular as many of his tries, but only he would have squeezed in at the left-hand corner. Jonathan Davies failed with a difficult conversion, but Widnes had a one-point advantage and just a few minutes injury-time to preserve their precious lead.

From the re-start Wigan kicked to Offiah's wing, and unbelievably Martin usually so sure-handed, knocked on. Perhaps he was still on a high and lost concentration after his superb try. From the ensuing scrum Wigan got the ball and in the last set of six of the game were awarded a disputable - to say the least - penalty. Following the intervention of a touch-judge, Darren Wright was penalised for an imaginary high tackle on Wigan's New Zealand centre Dean Bell. I say imaginary, because Wright never made any contact with Bell's head at all. He could not have done, because Bell had been leg-tackled by another Widnes defender.

Showing maturity beyond his years, Bobby Goulding kicked the penalty and in effect kicked Widnes out of contention for the 1989/90 Championship. Darren Wright's disciplinary record in 10 years at Widnes was almost as impeccable as his defence. In contrast, Dean Bell was something of a 'hitman' and indeed was suspended in the 1989/90 season. Darren had been featured the previous week in the match-programme for the Challenge Cup tie against Batley. It was ironic and perhaps truthful what he stated in the programme:

"The thing about the cup is a lot of the games are televised and referees feel they have to punish the slightest indiscretion, whereas if the games aren't on TV they tend to show more leniency. Everybody at Widnes knows that we have to keep our tackles low - it's been drilled into us."

In the February 8th edition of the *WWN* Doug Laughton wrote:

"All told it was a somewhat disturbing seven days for yours truly last week. No doubt, like me, many readers were disillusioned by the incident resulting in the penalty that gave Wigan victory. I have seen it on the video and I feel particularly sorry for Darren Wright who had such a magnificent game. Many people have said we must do something about the incident."

The Club did indeed act by sending a report to RL headquarters on the referee Colin Morris, and on the intervening touch-judge. Perhaps the trauma and disappointment of the last-minute defeat to Wigan affected the Chemics form in their next game. They were again drawn at home to another Second Division team in the second round of the Challenge Cup. They progressed to the third round, but were again unconvincing as they laboured to a 22-16 victory over Rochdale Hornets. The *WWN* match-report by Paul Cook was headlined **"Chemics struggle to find their top gear"**. The headline would have been apt for several games since the WCC victory over Canberra back in October. Something like top gear was found in the next league fixture at home to Hull on February 18th. Widnes displayed much of their old flair and authority in a 34-12 victory which included yet another Offiah hat-trick. The match-report headlines this time were: **"Scent of success is in the air"** alluding to the possibility of reaching the Challenge Cup Final.

The Chemics were drawn at home again in the third round. They were to face Oldham another Second division side on February 25th. If the form against Hull was repeated a place in the semi-final was assured. A new electronic scoreboard which had been installed at Naughton Park showed a depressing, almost unbelievable scoreline at the end of the game. It displayed Widnes 4 Oldham 16. Widnes were beaten by underdogs who played like men possessed, particularly their captain and loose-forward John Cogger. Playing with a strong wind in the first-half, the Chemics went ahead with two Jonathan Davies penalty goals. They were to be the only points scored as Oldham stifled both the mobile Widnes forwards and high-speed backline. Even Martin Offiah was limited to one running chance in the first-half. Perhaps the defeat was an accident waiting to happen after the laboured performances in the previous two rounds.

How could it have happened? There were only two changes from the side that thrashed the Australian champions in October. And missing from the side against Canberra Raiders was the mighty Emosi Koloto. He was now back after his early-season injury. The exit from the 1990 Challenge Cup, really was a bitter disappointment. Virtually out the Championship race and with the controversial defeats in 1988 and 89 surely still in the collective memory, there was all the incentive to reach the 1990 final. The *WWN* report of the Oldham debacle began:

"The new scoreboard flashed information throughout Sunday's Silk Cut Challenge Cup quarter-final at Naughton Park. But all its electronic wizardry could not begin to explain Widnes' erratic season. Had a computer been fed the Chemics were entertaining a Second Division side - it would surely have predicted a home win. But this has been a season to defy those who look into the future."

The hang-over from the shock Challenge Cup exit seemed to last for nearly all of the month of March. Two draws at Wakefield on March 4th and at Leigh on March 18th 10-10 and 20-20 respectively, were interspersed with a 22-30 defeat at Featherstone, and a thrashing at home by Bradford Northern. The new scoreboard at the end of the game displayed a another unbelievable scoreline, Widnes 14 Bradford Northern 40. The draw at Wakefield was scraped by a last-minute Darren Wright try and a touch-line conversion by Jonathan Davies. The draw at Leigh was marred by the sending-off of Emosi Koloto. The giant Tongan became the fifth Widnes player to be sent off in the 1989/90 season. A remarkable statistic given that Darren Wright had stated it had been drilled into the players not to tackle high! At Leigh Paul Moriarty did a good job as stand-in goalkicker. He kicked four and almost won the game three minutes from time with a 55-yard penalty that just failed wide. He also scored one the three Widnes tries, the other two being shared by David and Paul Hulme.

Not enough and too late

THE new scoreboard flashed information throughout Sunday's Silk Cut Challenge Cup quarter-final at Naughton Park.

But all its electronic wizardry could not begin to explain Widnes' erratic season.

PAUL GRANT AT

Widnes 4pts
Oldham 10pts

NAUGHTON PARK

were rewarded with a try from Henderson. They went further ahead with a Platt pen alty before Offiah with his only touch of the half raced through to the line after tapping a ball through the defence. But an Oldham player managed to kick the ball away before Offiah could make the touchdown.

A half-time dressing down by Dou[Laughton immediately sparked great effor from Chemics.

Prior to the last game of the month at Wigan of all places, Doug had signed Halifax forward Les Holliday. Laughton stated in the *WWN* that it would be "nice to throw a spanner in the Wigan works." Few would have given his stuttering team any chance of doing so. The Chemics had not won in five games and their form since the World Club Championship victory was that of a mid-table team. In all competitions, they had won 12, drawn two and lost 12 of 26 games. The night after Widnes had defeated Canberra Raiders, Wigan had also lost to Second Division Oldham away in the semi-final of the Lancashire Cup. Since then they had lost just two and drawn one of 27 games, winning their last eight. They had won the John Player Trophy, virtually wrapped up the Championship and had reached the Challenge Cup Final. The form-book was thrown away as a resurgent Widnes team pulled off a 24-9 victory. Flying Scotsman Alan Tait scored a hat-trick of tries, but the *WWN* match report highlighted the display of debutant Les Holliday and the try he set up for David Hulme. The report commenced:

"One flash of brilliance from Les Holliday nine minutes from the end of the match was more than enough to suggest that Widnes did the right thing in laying out £100,000 for his services. A deft dummy and a quick change of direction put Holliday in the clear 15 yards out and his perfect pass enabled the stand-off to score a crucial try.

That magical move by Widnes gave fans a glimpse of exactly what the team has been missing this season. Holliday at first receiver freed David Hulme to his best roving role and for 40 second half minutes Widnes looked like the team of old. Alan Tait took all the plaudits for his first hat-trick of tries, but this was a real team performance with hardly a weak link to be seen."

The Chemics were back on track! The strings of wins that Doug Laughton said was needed after the Challenge Cup defeat by Oldham had belatedly begun. It was apt that Sheffield Eagles were the visitors to Naughton Park on April 1st. It was the Eagles who had knocked Doug's team off their pedestal after winning the World Club Championship. A born-again Widnes paid Sheffield back with interest and handed out a 52-20 thrashing. Darren Wright was the hat-trick man this time displaying all his pace and class. His co-centre Andy Currier back after suspension also helped himself to two tries, as did hooker Phil McKenzie. One of McKenzie's tries in the second-half was the pick of the 11 scored. Les Holliday showing again his skills, chipped over the Sheffield defence, Alan Tait picked up Holliday's kick at pace and then sent McKenzie over. The Scotsman also helped himself to a try to add to his three at Wigan.

In the aftermath of winning the World Club Championship, the Chemics also lost heavily in the Lancashire Cup semi-final at Warrington. They also avenged this defeat on Good Friday with a 22-10 victory at Wilderspool. A 34-16 drubbing of St Helens at Naughton Park on East Monday in their last league fixture gave them their fourth successive victory and a third-place finish in Division One. New signing Les Holliday continued his great form against Warrington and St Helens. He seemed to have "freshened things up". John Devereux on the right-wing was in great from and had scored a try in each of the last three games. Devereux was selected along with Tait. Davies and Offiah for the Great Britain squad that toured New Zealand and Papa New Guinea in the summer of 1990. Martin who did not score in the win at Wigan, never played in the last three games. His absence gave even more merit to the late-season surge.

Doug Laughton's team were clearly in the mood for a tilt at retaining the Premiership Trophy. The 'feel good' factor was back, though perhaps not for stalwart Mike O'Neill who was transfer-listed in April 1990. In the first round of the Premiership Trophy Widnes were to confront Hull at Naughton Park on April 22nd. In the match-programme both Doug Laughton and Tony Myler expressed their concern and need for the aforementioned Great Britain tour to New Zealand and Papa New Guinea. The Hulme brothers and several players from other clubs most notably Ellery Hanley, had declined selection for the tour. The Chemics prevailed by 18 points to 8 as opposed to 18-10 at Old Trafford in the 1989 final. As in the previous year's final, Widnes could not turn their dominance into a landslide. Indeed, the headline of the *WWN* match-report was **"Chemics win marred by several wasted opportunities for scoring."**

Championship runners-up Leeds had to be overcome in the semi-final at Headingley a fortnight later if Widnes were to reach Old Trafford again. They started a disastrously by conceding a try in the second minute. Leeds international stand-off Gary Schofield hoisted a bomb which confused both Alan Tait and Martin Offiah. Leeds centre Rob Ackerman took advantage of the confusion to give his team an early advantage. It was a scrappy, stop-start first half littered with dropped passes and free-kicks. By the interval the Chemics had forged a 10-7 lead courtesy of a Jonathan Davies obstruction try and two penalties and a conversion by the Welsh Wizard.

Chemics' win marred by several wasted opportunities for scoring

WIDNES' Premiership express is speeding towards a third successive final.

But it could have so easily have come off the rails at the first stop.

For the Chemics' tough performance was marred by a number of wasted scoring opportunities which could have cost them dear.

But thankfully, for once this season, lady luck was shining on the black and white shirts.

PAUL GRANT

**Widnes 18pts
Hull 8pts**

at Naughton Park

In the second-half Widnes scored 20 unanswered points consisting of three tries, two goals and a drop-goal by that man Les Holliday. Jonathan Davies playing on the right-wing set up the second Widnes try in the 52nd minute. Fielding a Leeds drop-out in his own half, he ripped through the Leeds defence before feeding Andy Currier who carried on the attack before passing to Phil McKenzie to complete the 60-yard move. The next try demonstrated the handling skills of Holliday and Emosi Koloto as they sent Richie Eyres over. The third try was best of the three. Tony Myler on as a second-half substitute, gave a deft, delayed pass to Darren Wright again in the Widnes half. Darren tore through the Myler-made gap before passing to Martin Offiah when he reached the Leeds 25. Martin sped away from two Leeds defenders to score in the corner and sealed a 27-7 victory. Martin had also scored a try on his return to the side against Hull in the first round. Returning to the side against Leeds was Mike O'Neill. He showed he still had a lot to offer. Part of the match-report read:

"Emosi Koloto, Richie Eyres and Mike O'Neill pummelled the Leeds defence while captain Kurt Sorensen never missed a tackle."

Doug Laughton's born-again team were on a real roll and favourites to beat Bradford Northern in the 1990 Premiership Final. Even so, his *WWN* column on May 10th three days before the showdown was headlined **"CHEMICS WIN BY NO MEANS SURE."** Doug highlighted the trouncing Bradford had given his team at Naughton Park in March, and also the fact they had defeated Wigan in the semi-final. He named an unchanged side from the one that had won so brilliantly at Leeds in the semi-final. Therefore, transfer-listed Mike O'Neill after his impressive display at Headingley retained his place. Surprisingly, there was no place on the right-wing for the emerging John Devereux. Jonathan Davies was again in that position has he had been at Leeds, and indeed in the 1989 Premiership Final. Showing only two changes from the team that played in the final the previous year, the Widnes line-up against Bradford was:

Alan Tait, Jonathan Davies, Andy Currier, Darren Wright, Martin Offiah, David Hulme, Paul Hulme, Kurt Sorensen, Phil McKenzie, Mike O'Neill, Richie Eyres, Emosi Koloto, Les Holliday, Substitutes: Tony Myler and Joe Grima.

In complete contrast to the semi-final, it was Widnes who scored in the second minute. Slick inter-passing between Tait and Holliday led to the signing from Halifax going over for his first try for the Club. Jonathan Davies tagged over an easy conversion to give Widnes an early 6-0 lead. In the 26th minute the Flying Scotsman made the Bradford defence look static as he scored the second try himself. His effort was not converted, but the Chemics looked in control as half-time approached. Then right on the interval a potentially lethal blow was dealt to the Widnes team. Paul Hulme was sent-off for alleged gouging, and a 10-point lead was by no means a winning one. Some Widnes supporters may have been haunted by memories of the loss to St Helens in the previous year's Challenge Cup semi-final when Richie Eyres was sent-off.

Though a man down, the Chemics went on the offensive and scored three more tries in the second-half. Tony Myler again came on as a substitute and helped et up the first. The Maestro made a break to put his side in an attacking position from which Alan Tait scored his second try. Soon after Tait set up Andy Currier for a try and then Currier scored his own second. With 15 minutes still remaining the game was in the bag at 26-0. Northern scored a converted try, Jonathan Davies kicked a penalty to make the final score 28-6. Widnes had become the first team to win the Premiership Trophy in three successive seasons. Once again, captain Kurt Sorensen was lifting the Premiership Trophy to the cheers of Widnes fans at Manchester United's famous ground. The King had actually been substituted at half-time. Perhaps it was a tactical switch by Doug Laughton in the context of Paul Hulme's sending-off.

The victory was perhaps particularly satisfying for Alan Tait, Mike O'Neill and Andy Currier. Tait won the Harry Sunderland trophy for being voted player-of-the-match for the second successive year. Mike O'Neill had won his sixth Premiership Trophy medal. His first was almost 10 years to the day also against Bradford Northern. Mike and Bradford full-back Keith Mumby were the only players who played in both the 1980 and 1990 finals. Mike stated in the WWN the following week that he wanted to stay at Widnes. As it transpired, the 1990 Premiership Final was his last game for the Club. He had been a great servant who had also featured in four Challenge Cup Finals for the 'Cup Kings' between 1979 and 1984. Andy Currier's two tries ended a turbulent season on a high after being barracked by home supporters in October, and serving an eight-match suspension rather unfairly in March and April.

RECORD BREAKERS! Mike O'Neill, the Widnes forward who won his sixth Premiership Final winners medal and (right) full back Alan Tait, double try scorer and the only player to receive the Man of the Match award twice.

The headline for the match-report in the *WWN* was **"Superb Chemics win sixth Premiership title."** and began:

"A superb twelve-man second half performance from Widnes took them to their sixth Premiership Trophy, and a record third in succession, beating Bradford 28-6 at Old Trafford on Sunday. The Chemics were forced to play the second half a man down after scrum half Paul Hulme was given his marching orders seconds before the half time hooter. But coach Doug Laughton calmed his troops at half time and made an inspired substitution replacing Kurt Sorensen with Tony Myler."

A third-place finish in Division One and another Premiership Trophy would have been a season of great success at other clubs. For this Widnes team it was one of under-achievement. Their main rivals Wigan had won the two major trophies, namely the Championship and the Challenge Cup. They had also retained the newly-named Regal Trophy. Doug Laughton's super-fast and super-talented team lost focus for much of the season before their late rally which culminated at Old Trafford. Could they knock Wigan off their perch in the 1990/91 season? They were certainly more consistent only dropping 12 league points as against 18 in the 1989/90 season. They were in the Championship race right to the end, but sadly fell at the last hurdle. They also had a much better Challenge Cup campaign in 1991 but again fell at the last hurdle before Wembley.

Worse however, was the news that broke on the morning of their fourth successive Premiership Final. It was to be a sad end to a season that had promised so much.

A triumphant Widnes team after winning a third successive Premiership Final in 1990.

Fixtures, results, attendances and points scorers 1989/90 season

Opposition	Venue	Result	Attend.	Goals	Tries
AUGUST					
27 Wigan (Charity Shield)	Liverpool	27-22	5,044	Davies (5), Tait dg	Kebbie, Davies, Offiah, D. Hulme
SEPTEMBER					
4 Salford	Home	**46- 8**	8,591	**Davies (7)**	**Offiah (2), P. Hulme, Kebbie, Davies, Sorensen, Grima, Koloto**
11 Hull	Away	26-11	8,298	Davies (3)	Offiah (2), Kebbie, Myler, O'Neill
17 Carlisle (Lancashire Cup 1)	Away	46- 6	4,329	Davies (5)	Kebbie (4), Davies (2), Offiah, McKenzie, Koloto
24 Featherstone Rovers	Home	**59- 8**	8,008	**Davies (9), Tait dg**	**Kebbie (4), Offiah (4), McKenzie, Davies**
27 Leigh (Lancashire Cup 2)	Away	34-12	6,748	Davies (5)	Offiah (2), Tait (2), D. Hulme, Davies
OCTOBER					
4 Canberra Raiders (World Club Championship)	Manchester	30-18	30,786	Davies (3)	Offiah (2), P. Hulme, Davies, Eyres Wright
8 Sheffield Eagles	Away	6-31	8,636	Davies	McKenzie
10 Warrington (Lancashire Cup semi)	Away	6-28	10,240	Davies	Currier
15 Wakefield Trinity	Home	**30-12**	7,488	**Davies (5)**	**Offiah (3), P. Hulme. Currier**
31 Salford	Away	28-16	5,453	Davies (4)	Currier (2), Offiah, Kebbie, Smith
NOVEMBER					
5 New Zealand (Tour Game)	Home	**18-26**	9,905	**Davies**	**Tait, D. Hulme,,O'Neill, Kebbie**
12 Leigh	Home	**16-18**	7,104	**Davies (4)**	**Tait, O'Neill**
19 Leeds	Away	**12-26**	14,111	**Davies (2)**	**Offiah (2)**
25 Castleford	Home	**24-16**	5,122	**Davies (4)**	**Currier, Sorensen, Devereux, Davies**
DECEMBER					
3 Nottingham (Regal Trophy 1)	Away	48-18	2,246	Davies (3), Currier (3)	Kebbie (3), Offiah (2), Currier, Davies, McKenzie, P. Hulme
9 Wigan (Regal Trophy 2)	Away	0-18	12,398		
17 Barrow	Away	34- 4	2,124	Currier (7)	Sorenson (2), Devereux, Davies,
20 Barrow	Home	**48- 0**	3,782	**Currier (6)**	**Devereux (2), McKenzie (2), Critchley, Tait, D. Hulme, Currier, Offiah**
26 Warrington	Home	**32-20**	10,179	**Currier (4)**	**Offiah (3), Devereux (2), Eyres**
JANUARY					
1 St Helens	Away	18- 8	12,375	Davies (3)	Davies (2), Tait
7 Leeds	Home	**8-20**	10,232	**Currier (2)**	**P. Hulme**
17 Bradford Northern	Away	6-16	5,279	Davies	Moriarty
20 Castleford	Away	30-22	5,203	Currier (3)	Offiah (4), Currier, P. Hulme
28 Batley (Challenge Cup 1)	Home	**26-10**	5,801	**Currier (2), Tait**	**Tait, Devereux, Offiah, D. Hulme, O'Neill**
FEBRUARY					
3 Wigan	Home	**10-11**	9,542	**Davies**	**Marsh, Offiah**
11 Rochdale Hornets (Challenge Cup 2)	Home	**22-16**	6,546	**Davies (3)**	**Davies, Devereux, O'Neill, Offiah**
18 Hull	Home	**30-12**	7,356	**Davies (3)**	**Offiah (3), Tait, Wright, McKenzie**
25 Oldham (Challenge Cup 3)	Home	**4-11**	11,802	**Davies (2)**	
MARCH					
4 Wakefield Trinity	Away	10-10	5,203	Davies	Davies, Wright
7 Featherstone Rovers	Away	22-30	3,525	Davies (3)	Moriarty, Tait, Davies, Devereux
11 Bradford Northern	Home	**14-40**	6,805	**Moriarty**	**Offiah (2), Wright**
18 Leigh	Away	20-20	4,848	Moriarty (4)	P. Hulme, Moriarty, D. Hulme
24 Wigan	Away	22- 8	10,916	Currier (3)	Tait (3), D. Hulme
APRIL					
1 Sheffield Eagles	Home	**52-20**	6,212	**Currier (4)**	**Wright (3), Currier (2), McKenzie (2), Tait, Marsh, Devereux, D. Hulme**
13 Warrington	Away	22-10	7,740	Davies (3)	McKenzie, Wright, Eyres, Devereux
16 St Helens	Home	**34-16**	11,931	**Davies (7)**	**Devereux, Currier, D. Hulme, Grima, Davies**
22 Hull (Premiership 1)	Home	**18- 8**	8,672	**Currier (3)**	**Tait, Koloto, Offiah**
MAY					
6 Leeds (Premiership 2)	Away	27- 7	17,082	Davies (5), Holliday dg	Davies, McKenzie, Eyres, Offiah
13 Bradford Northern (Premiership Final)	Manchester	28- 6	40,796	Davies (4)	Tait (2), Currier (2), Holliday

Players total number of games and points 1989/90 season

	Played	Goals	Tries	Points
Chris Ashurst	4			0
Jason Critchley	10		1	4
Andy Currier	27	37	13	126
Jonathan Davies	30	98	16	260
John Devereux	25		12	48
Barry Dowd	5			0
Andy Eyres	2			0
Richie Eyres	32		4	16
Joe Grima	32		2	8
Les Holliday	7	(1dg)	1	5
David Hulme	38		10	40
Paul Hulme	26		6	24
Brimah Kebbie	16		16	64
Emosi Koloto	19		3	12
David Marsh	16		2	8
Phil McKenzie	37		11	44
Paul Moriarty	24	5	3	22
Tony Myler	30		1	4
Mike O'Neill	28		3	12
Martin Offiah	32		40	160
Derek Pyke	24			0
Mark Sarsfield	1			0
David Smith	24		1	4
Kurt Sorensen	31		4	16
Stuart Spruce	1			0
Alan Tait	36	(2dg) 1	17	72
Boblyn Tuavao	1			0
Darren Wright	32		8	32

First Division	Games	Won	Drawn	Lost	For	Against	Points
Wigan	26	20	0	6	699	349	40
Leeds	26	18	0	8	704	383	36
Widnes	26	16	2	8	659	423	34
Bradford Northern	26	17	0	9	614	416	34
St Helens	26	17	0	9	544	170	34
Hull	26	16	1	9	577	400	33
Castleford	26	16	0	10	703	448	32
Warrington	26	13	1	12	424	451	27
Wakefield Trinity	26	12	1	13	502	528	25
Featherstone Rovers	26	10	0	16	479	652	20
Sheffield Eagles	26	9	1	16	517	588	19
Leigh	26	9	1	16	442	642	19
Salford	26	4	1	21	421	699	9
Barrow	26	1	0	25	201	1133	2

5) 1990/91 season "The departure of Doug"

Prior to the start of the 1990/91 season the Club reported a loss of £62,000. This was in part due to a fall in average attendances from 8,648 to 7,958. The main factor though was the steep rise in players wages. This financial loss was incurred despite the close season sales not only of Mike O'Neill to Rochdale, but also Derek Pyke to Oldham. In contrast to O'Neill, Pyke had only been at the Club for two years. He had though been another astute purchase by Doug Laughton, and had shown his experience and subtle handling skills in his 66 first-team appearances. Remarkably he did not score a single try in those 66 games. Not that he needed to with so many speedsters playing alongside him. Pyke certainly had a hand in many spectacular Widnes tries in his time at the Club. He had actually been injured and lost his place in the team late in the 1989/90 season.

Could the Chemics carry the superb form in the last seven games of the 1989/90 season into the new one? They certainly could. They made a real statement of intent for the 1990/91 season by defeating their main rivals Wigan twice in the first three games. They defeated them again in the Charity Shield and in the second round of the Lancashire Cup at Naughton Park. The scorelines were 21-5 and 24-22 respectively. In between the two Wigan games, they had travelled to Whitehaven in the first round of the Lancashire Cup and massacred the Second Division team by 70 points to 6. Jonathan Davies in particular, made a statement of intent for the season by scoring eight tries and kicking 17 goals over the three games!

Despite Doug Laughton suggesting that the Charity Shield should annually be played at Anfield a year earlier, it was played in 1990 at Swansea. On his return to Wales, Jonathan Davies scored a hat trick of tries of and kicked two goals. A Whitehaven, after scoring a try at Swansea, Martin Offiah scored his first hat-trick of the season. Jonathan did even better and scored four tries in addition to kicking nine goals. Both players scored a try each in the Lancashire Cup victory over Wigan on September 2nd. It was a late Davies penalty goal that enabled the Chemics to progress to the semi-final. The *WWN* match-report headline read: "**FAULTLESS DISPLAY FROM DAVIES**" and the report began:

"Is there any stopping Jonathan Davies this season? A match-winning performance in the Charity Shield, a club record points total against Whitehaven and now a 16-point haul to put Widnes into the Lancashire Cup semi-finals against Warrington."

After his flying start to the 1990/91 season, 'Jiffy' was stopped in his tracks in the Chemics next six games. He never scored a single try although continued to bang over the goals. On September 9th Widnes commenced their league fixtures with a 14-10 away victory at Bradford. It was a hard-fought win and there were just two Widnes tries, both scored by the ever-consistent Darren Wright. Martin Offiah missed the Bradford game and the next three games because of a ligament injury. Doug gave a debut in his place to Harvey Howard who subsequently developed into a formidable forward. St Helens coach Alex Murphy as controversial as ever, had a column in the *Daily Mirror* in which he stated that Widnes were an ordinary side without Martin. The following Wednesday evening the Chemics were to play

Warrington in the Lancashire Cup semi-final as they had done in 1989. In 1990 home advantage was with Widnes. David Hulme in his testimonial year, would write in the match-programmes during the 90/'91 season as Tony Myler had done the previous year. In the programme for the encounter with Warrington he dismissed Alex Murphy's opinion stating:

"I notice recently a certain coach and columnist in the Daily Mirror said that without Martin in our side we an ordinary team. I'm sorry Alex but I can't agree. Whilst I would agree that we obviously miss Martin, after all he is the best in the business, I think that we have a side loaded with talent and pace, capable of making a very successful run this term."

David was vindicated as the Chemics reversed the defeat by Warrington in the 1989 Lancashire Cup semi-final with an impressive 22-4 victory. The following Sunday they defeated Featherstone Rovers 41-14 at in the first home league fixture of the season. Not only Offiah who had scored four tries in the fixture the two previous seasons was out injured, so were the Hulme brothers and Tony Myler. The half-back positions and one prop-forward position were filled by three players with only a handful of first-team appearances between them. Andy Eyres the younger brother of Richie, Stuart Spruce and Chris Ashurst all played impressively. Andy Eyres scored his only two tries for Widnes against Featherstone. The *WWN* report praised the performances of the three players but also expressed concern about the attendance, it read:

"Half-backs Andy Eyres and Stuart Spruce plus front rower Chris Ashurst gave everything to ensure the likes of David Hulme and Tony Myler weren't missed.

If no more than 6,566 spectators on a fine September afternoon to watch this side play then Heaven help Widnes in January and February. You can't ask for more than the Chemics have delivered this season - Charity Shield winners, Lancashire Cup finalists, twice victors over Wigan - and yet the fans still stay away."

Jonathan Davies was on the cover of the programme for the 1990 Charity Shield game at Swansea. It was apt as he kicked two goals and scored three tries on his return to Wales.

Three years earlier as recalled in the second chapter of this book, Doug Laughton had also asked "where are the fans?". That was when less than 4,000 spectators were at Naughton Park to see his unbeaten side defeat Hull Kingston Rovers. An attendance of 6,566 may have been acceptable in 1987, but in 1990 after two Championships, three Premiership triumphs and a World Club Championship victory, expectations were higher. More significantly, expenses were higher, in particular players wages and contracts. The Chemics flying start to the season came to an abrupt halt as it had done in the 1989/90 season after winning the World Club Championship. On September 23rd they lost their first game of the 1990/91 season by an almost identical 6-31 scoreline. Hull scored a point more than what Sheffield did in the previous season. Perhaps Doug Laughton's men had an eye on the forthcoming Lancashire Cup Final.

The 1990 final was to be played at Wigan's Central Park ground. Widnes were to play Salford who had been relegated from the First Division at the end of the 1989/90 season. It was perhaps an omen that the decade-long reign of 'The Cup Kings' had begun in the 1974 final also against Salford at Central Park. The Chemics had Martin Offiah back on the left-wing and surprisingly Darren Wright was selected on the right-wing ahead of John Deveruex. Kurt Sorensen had relinquished the captaincy at the start of the 1990/91 season. Not that it made much difference, Kurt still led from the front no matter what. Tony Myler was captain of the team to face Salford. The Widnes line-up was:

Alan Tait. Darren Wright, Andy Currier, Jonathan Davies, Martin Offiah, Tony Myler, David Hulme, Kurt Sorensen, Phil McKenzie, Chris Ashurst, Richie Eyres, Emosi Koloto, Les Holliday, Substitutes: **John Devereux and David Smith.**

The opening exchanges were lively and pretty even. After 10 minutes Jonathan Davies slotted over a penalty to give his side the lead. It was short-lived as Alan Tait made a hash of kicking into touch a kick ahead by a Salford player near his own line. Salford centre Peter Williams picked the ball up and scored an unconverted try to give his side a 4-2 lead. Widnes hit back with two tries in which Andy Currier was instrumental. First, Andy intercepted a Salford passing move and raced 60 yards to score an unconverted try Then in a reversal of customary roles, he executed a clever off-load for Tony Myler to score near the posts. Jonathan Davies added an easy conversion to put Widnes 12-4 in front. By half-time the underdogs were level thanks to a penalty goal and a converted try by their skipper Ian Blease.

In the first 10 minutes of the second-half Widnes almost scored two spectacular tries. Jonathan Davies made a great jinking run from his own 25. Reaching the half-way line, he handed on to the supporting Phil McKenzie who in turn fed Alan Tait linking up from the full-back position. The Scotsman kicked ahead, but the ball rolled dead. It was a breath-taking passage of play that prompted Clive Tyldesley in his television commentary to exclaim, "It had Widnes written all over it". The second effort also had Widnes written all over it and more specifically Martin Offiah written all over it. Martin popped up on the right side of the field and scythed through from just inside his own half. He would have scored in the right-hand corner but put a foot into touch.

Against the run-of-play Salford then scored a great try to take the lead. They took the Widnes defence by surprise and ran the ball on the sixth tackle. Left-winger Adrian Hadley burst down the flank and fed supporting stand-off Graham Fell who scored a converted try. An upset looked on as the underdogs still held an 18-12 lead with less than 15 minutes remaining. Then from close-range, Widnes substitute forward David Smith took a Kurt Sorensen pass to plunge over for a converted try which equalised the scores. And with two minutes remaining Martin Offiah who else! got a winning try. Phil McKenzie made a typical run from acting half-back, fed Martin who again from close-range bounced off one defender, forced his way past another to clinch a hard-earned victory.

In contrast to the World Club Championship triumph the previous season, two successive home league victories followed. Oldham were beaten 24-16 and Castleford were thrashed 46-4. The respective headlines of the match-reports in the *WWN* **"CHEMICS REGAIN OLD FORM - FOR THE FIRST HALF HOUR"** and **"Castleford feel full force of Chemic's best"**, reflected the two Widnes performances. Castleford coach Malcolm Reilly was also the coach of Great Britain who were shortly to play Australia in the 1990 Ashes series. Martin Offiah was an automatic selection and showed why with another great hat-trick of tries. Martin had also scored against Oldham and had now scored in every one of the six games he had played in the 1990/91 season. Several Widnes players made a point about their omissions from the squad for the first Test. The *WWN* match-reporter Paul Cook noted:

"Tony Myler, David Hulme, Phil McKenzie, Richard Eyres and Andy Currier put over their argument for inclusion in the international line-up."

SPORT

Lancs Cup finally comes to Widnes

WELL Widnes finally did it, but Salford put up a display that suggested they will have much more to offer in the First Division next season than they have for many years.

And it was a good job that the Chemics shrugged off their attacking torpor when they did, because any criticism of the referee...

WIDNES 24pts SALFORD 18pts

By Paul Cook

run at the heart of the Salford defence that showed the markers up just enough for him to release a pass to David Smith and the young prop crashed over under the posts.

Davies pulled and Widnes were level although after earlier having lead 12-4 there should have been no need for them to come back.

and in attempting to kick it into touch he missed the ball completely and Peter Williams followed up to score.

The Chemics were having to fight for every yard at this stage but looked to be in command with two tries in a five-minute burst.

First Andy Currier intercepted a Fell pass to race 50 yards and touch down, and then he set up Tony Myler for a try between the posts to which Davies added the two...

Cheers! Emosi Koloto celebrates Widnes' Lancashire Cup

Doug Laughton's column in the programme for the Castleford game was headlined **"KURT...ONE OF THE GREAT WIDNES SKIPPERS"**. Doug explained in the programme his reasons for relinquishing Kurt Sorensen from the captaincy. Kurt it seems had told Doug it would his final playing season. He was also going to be unavailable in October as he was going to Australia for his sister's wedding. The King also had business interests the legendary *Top of The Town* night-club in partnership with Jim Mills. I cannot fathom why co-running a night-club would have been a factor in a captaincy decision! Whatever, Kurt did not take a huff and as already written still carried on leading from the front.

New skipper Tony Myler seemed to be relishing the role. He had been in great form and scored two more tries at Hull Kingston Rovers on October 14th. Jonathan Davies also ended his try-drought at Hull K.R. but the Chemics lost narrowly 20-22. The defeat was a blip as the Chemics returned to winning ways at Wakefield the following week. Jonathan Davies now back in the try-scoring groove scored two more in a 16-6 victory. Martin Offiah had drawn his first blanks of the season at Hull K.R and Wakefield. Jonathan therefore had regained his position as leading try-scorer by the end of October. He had scored 11 to Martin's 9, but Martin had played four games less.

Widnes had no fixture in the last weekend of October because the first Test between Great Britain and Australia was contested at Wembley which the hosts won 19-12. The first fixture in November was a televised league game at Naughton Park against Leeds. The 20-8 Leeds victories of the two previous seasons were not repeated. The classy Chemics reversed the scoreline of the two previous seasons and added another six to win 26-8. It was a travesty that Leeds had four players selected for the previous week's Test, whilst Widnes had only Martin Offiah in the GB team. Martin scored one of the Widnes tries as did Kurt Sorensen after his sojourn in October. Kurt was substituted at half-time for fellow Kiwi forward Esene Faimalo to make his first home appearance. Faimalo was to prove to be another good signing by Doug. There was no fixture either the week after the Leeds game. The second Test was played at Old Trafford and Australia equalised the series with a last-gasp try to win 14-10.

Before the third deciding Test, the Aussies were to play Doug Laughton's team on November 18th. The Widnes team of 1978 were the last British last Club side to beat an Australian touring team. There was an attendance of 14,666 for the game, which was previewed on the front-page of the November 15th edition of the *WWN* with the headline **"MATCH OF THE YEAR"**. The Chemics lost 8-15, but the seven-point margin reflected how hard the tourists had to work for victory. The game was played in rainy and windy conditions. The Aussies won the toss and chose to play with the wind and rain behind them in the first-half. The Chemics were only 0-6 down when on the stroke half-time, Dale Shearer who had played for Widnes three seasons earlier, scored a controversial unconverted try.

With the wind and rain at their backs in the second-half the Chemics pressed strongly. Jonathan Davies had kicked a 40-yard penalty to reduce the 10-point deficit, and Sorensen, Grima and Faimalo got close to scoring tries. Then against the run of play and against the wind and rain Mal Maninga made a telling break to send his right-winger Greg Alexander in at the corner for an unconverted try. It should have killed Widnes off, but with five minutes left, Tony Myler sent Jonathan Davies in who converted his own effort to put his side in with an outside chance of a draw. As it happened, the Australian full-back Gary Belcher had the final say with a drop-goal right at the death.

The Saturday after defeating Widnes, the Australians also defeated Great Britain 14-0 at Elland Road Leeds to retain the Ashes. Jonathan Davies was the substitute back for Great Britain and David Hulme was also added to the GB squad for the third Test but not selected. Martin Offiah had played in all three Tests. Jonathan and Martin both played for the Chemics the following day at Oldham. David Hulme did not play, and the scrum-half position was filled by Paul Hulme who had been injured since the opening game of the season against Wigan. Davies scored two tries and Offiah also scored one. It had been 11 games since the two leading try-scorers and superstars had scored a try in the same match. The other two Widnes tries in the 24-18 win at Oldham were scored by John Devereux and Darren Wright. Even though all five Widnes tries were scored by their three-quarters, the *WWN* report highlighted the "hard yards" made by the forwards and in particular the performance of Joe Grima. The fortunes and form of "Smokin Joe" had been transformed in the 12 months since the Club had considered cancelling his contract.

On the first three weekends in December, the first three rounds of the Regal Trophy were played. The Chemics took advantage of three home draws and moved through to the semi-finals with vintage performances. League leaders Hull and Leeds were beaten 24-16 and 22-6 respectively on successive Saturdays. Both games were televised by the BBC. Doug Laughton had commented previously about the amount of games involving his team that were televised. Indirectly alluding to the fact that television revenue did not compensate for diminished gate money, Doug was quoted as saying somewhat wryly "We may provide the nation with great entertainment but we have a club to run".

Richie Eyres in action against the Australian tourists at Naughton Park on November 18th 1990.

The Chemics certainly kept the nation entertained with some breath-taking tries in the two televised ties. To illustrate how the swashbuckling Widnes team would have thrilled the nation, it is perhaps worth including here how the *WWN* described four of the Widnes tries against Hull:

"John Devereux set the Widnes bandwagon rolling when he finished off a move that swept across field. Andy Currier primed him with a half-break and a lovely floated pass and Devereux sped down the wing crashing through Richard Day's tackle like a rhino charging a hunter's jeep. He picked himself up to score the second, again following a swift passing sequence with Currier once more supplying the final pass.

Devereux was involved in the third try, but it was Jonathan Davies's score all the way. On the fifth tackle he beat two Hull defenders with a couple of mesmerizing side-steps, accelerated clean away, fed Devereux on his outside and took the winger's return pass to race away under the posts. His goal made the score 14-10 at the break. In the second half Widnes cruised away to a 10-point lead when Martin Offiah beat Mackey all ends up for speed to go in at the corner and Davies kicked a wonderful conversion."

The third-round tie at home to Second Division Batley played on Sunday December 16th was not televised. There was an attendance of 6,656 to see the Second Division side thrashed 56-6. Yet only 3,466 and 4,940 respectively were at Naughton Park to see the victories over Hull and Leeds. In the match-programme for the home league game against Hull Kingston Rovers on the evening of December 19th Doug Laughton wrote:

"Last Sunday's game against Batley had many pleasing features, not least that we had the highest attendance of the Round which makes we wonder what sort of gate we would have had for the Hull and Leeds ties had they not been televised."

Hull K.R were also taken to the cleaners and thrashed 32-8. Martin Offiah who scored four tries aginst Batley, repeated the dose against Hull K.R. At last he had put some daylight between himself and Jonathan Davies as leading try-scorer. Martin had now scored 22 tries in just 14 games, whilst Jonathan had scored 17 tries in 19 games. As regular goal-kicker, the Welshman was the leading points-scorer and on course to break the Club's season points-scoring record. As with the team generally, Andy Currier had hit a purple patch in the sequence of home games in December. Though not scoring against Hull in the Regal Trophy first round, he scored six tries collectively against Leeds and Batley and in the league game against Hull K.R. The last two games of 1990 were both against Warrington. Widnes were to play at Wilderspool on Boxing Day, and in the Regal Trophy semi-final just two days later at Central Park. Over the Christmas period the *WWN* was published on Friday December 27th. A feature wriiten by reporter Denis Lancaster was headlined **"We can win the lot! "**. In his own column Doug wrote:

"We have one game left this year, the Regal Trophy semi-final against Warrington, and if we managed to win at Wilderspool yesterday, we can certainly do the business on Saturday. Thankfully, we go into 1991 in much better shape than we started 1990. Some may ask, what are our hopes and dreams for the next year?

Obviously, everyone is aching for another trip to Wembley and of course we would love to take the Championship back off Wigan. We would like to win the Regal Trophy and end up back at Old Trafford in the Premiership Final. Knowledgeable folk within the game would say that is dreaming in fine style. However, I do not think these are pipe dreams."

The Chemics did win the league game at Wilderspool, but could not repeat their hard-earned 8-2 victory in the Regal Trophy semi-final. Warrington almost reversed the scoreline and progressed to the final winning 8-4. The "Wires" tackled ferociously and deserved their victory. They were ahead at the interval by a single penalty goal. Early in the second-half another marvellous Martin Offiah try gave Widnes the lead. He took a forward-looking pass from Joe Grima and flew 60 yards along the touchline to score in the left-hand corner. Ten mnutes were remaining when Warrington drew level with a penalty goal, then their left-centre Chris Rudd scored a winning try. The hope of a 'Grand Slam' expressed by Doug Laughton was therefore dashed. It was a disappointment but not a disaster. Doug had implied in an earlier article that the League Championship was a greater priority than the Regal Trophy.

After defeating St Helens 14-8 at home on New Year's Day, the Chemics were poised to kick on to another Championship. They were Division One leaders on points difference over Hull and had a game in hand. They were five points clear of Wigan and were to play both at Naughton Park in January. By the end of the month the complexion of the Championship race had changed completely. On January 6th at Castleford Richie Eyres scored his first two tries of the season, but they were the only Widnes tries in a 10-22 defeat. The game against Hull scheduled for the following week was postponed. Wigan then came to Naughton Park on January 19th and gained two crucial league points that put them back in the Championship race. The 22-14 victory did not reflect Wigan's superiority as the Chemics scored one converted try in the last five minutes and another in injury time. Both were scored by Martin Offiah – the first from a cross-kick by Alan Tait, the second after a typical astute pass by Tony Myler - to put a false complexion on the scoreline. All three Wigan tries were scored by the awesome Ellery Hanley.

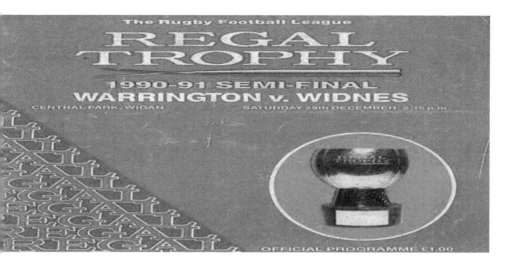

Doug Laughton's column in the programme for the New's Day game against St Helens was headed: **"DETERMINED THAT THE BAD TIMES WON'T RETURN."** alluding to the inconsistent form for much of the 1989/90 season. Some supporters may have concluded that it was no co-incidence that Jonathan Davies had not played in the last five games, three of which had been lost. The Welsh Wizard had been inspirational in the first-half of the 1990/91 season. The Chemics were to prove that bad times would not be returning - at least not immediately - and they had the speed and class to mask the absence of Davies. Jonathan's injury was to leave him side-lined for another six games. Bouncing back after the Wigan game, six emphatic victories were reeled off. By the end of February Widnes were still in the Championship race and had reached the third round of the Challenge Cup. A Championship, Challenge Cup and Premiership Trophy treble was still possible.

The sequence of victories began at Rochdale on the last Sunday in January. Richie Eyres scored three tries in a 60-6 slaughter adding to the couple he scored at Castleford. John Devereux playing in the left-centre position scored a brace as did Ben Eli playing in "Devs" more usual right-wing role. Eli was another signing from New Zealand, but it seems he was not quite good enough for this Widnes team. His two tries at Rochdale were the only two he scored in three first-team appearances. Amazingly, Martin Offiah did not score any of the Widnes tries at Rochdale Predictably, in the next game at Naughton Park he scored a hat-trick in a 34-6 rout of Wakefield Trinity. On February 3rd. Paul Cook highlighted what he thought were negative aspects of the victories over Rochdale and Wakefield. He wrote that Rochdale were "hopeless" and was also underwhelmed by the victory over Wakefield implying that some Widnes stars were out of form stating in the *WWN*:

"It may be that some players need shaking up a little to reproduce their best form. Certainly, the likes of Tait, Myler, the Hulme brothers and even Kurt Sorensen can play much better than they are at present. Tait still doesn't look like the player that once terrorised defences from the deep and Tony Myler shows to prove he's still got what it takes, but it has been coming too infrequently.

David and Paul Hulme can point to their Great Britain selection as proof of form but I doubt whether either would put his hand on his heart and say they were playing their best football. Kurt too, seems to have gone off the boil after a series of top-class pre-Christmas performances."

One man who may have disagreed with Cook's opinion about Sorensen's form was Jim Mills. In the programme for the Wakefield game Jim spoke about Kurt and stated:

"During his time as captain here at Widnes, I was very impressed with the way in which he showed great leadership to all around him. He led from the front. It's my opinion that we always seemed to play better when Kurt was out there in the middle, he was able to give us much needed direction and variation.

Of course, like us all Kurt won't mind me saying that he's not getting any younger, but it's strange that with the responsibility of captain being removed from him, he is for my money playing better than ever. I honestly think that he has a couple of good seasons left in him."

On February 10th the Chemics commenced their Challenge Cup campaign away at Second Division Doncaster. They eased through to the second round with a 30-4 victory. A fortnight later they brushed aside another Second Division side away to move through to the third round. Barrow were beaten by a similar score to Doncaster with the Chemics scoring just two points less than in the first round. The *WWN* headline for report on the Barrow game could well have applied also to the Doncaster game reading: **"Chemics in Cup Canter".** They were certainly a contrast to the first two rounds in 1990 against Second Division opposition. However, it was the two league games either side of the tie at Barrow that the intention to reach Wembley was clearly stated. Not only to reach Wembley, but to re-gain the Championship and retain the Premiership Trophy.

On February 17th Leeds were annihilated 38-0 at Headingley. and on the evening of February 27th, Championship rivals Hull were decisively beaten at home 28-2. The victory at Leeds ranks with the greatest Widnes performances in this era. In the previous season's Premiership semi- final, Martin Offiah had put the stamp on a convincing win by scoring a superb late try. In this latest hammering of Leeds on their home ground, he carried on from where he left off by scoring the opening Widnes try. Martin also carried on from where he left off at Headingley 24 hours earlier. He had scored five tries playing for Great Britain against France! Given the somewhat downbeat comments by *WWN* reporter Paul Cook after the Wakefield game on the form of the team and certain players, I thought it worthwhile quoting Cook's observation of the Leeds game and also Martin's opening try. His report began:

"Wonderful Widnes proved once again that Leeds bring out the best of them as they turned on by far their most convincing performance since the start of the year. Leeds were ripped to shreds by the flowing football that the rest of Division One fears. From full back to loose forward every player contributed to this Widnes win. Phil McKenzie's darting runs, Andy Currier's pace and strength plus Esene Faimalo's charges were the pick in what was an excellent team effort.

Chemics' comeback!

Leeds 0,
Widnes 38.

Report by
Paul Cook

Touchdown! Martin Offiah hits his sixth try of the weekend, this one against Leeds. following his five scores in Saturday's international. (C5390SB10)

Touchdown! Not one to miss out on a try scoring feast, John Devereu scores against Leeds on Sunday. (C5391SB19)

WONDERFUL Widnes proved once again that Leeds bring out the best in them as they turned in by far their most convincing performance since the start of the year.
In three meetings this season

with the Loiners, Widnes have cruised in for 86 points and conceded just 14 — impressive statistics when you consider that Leeds are the First Division's top scorers.

The Chemics wouldn't have been flattered by a score of 50 or 60 points such were the chances

that went begging. plus two certain tries the referee ruled out by stopping play when Widnes should have been given the advantage.

From the start, Widnes looked keener and sharper than they have done for weeks. There was an eagerness to get the job done and to do it in style.

End of an Era

When Widnes surrendered meekly to Wigan after blowing their big Regal Trophy chance against Warrington it looked as if the season might be turning sour in the second half. But the players have snapped back with a vengeance and with Emosi Koloto back in the side and Jonathan Davies fit again, what a run-in we have to look forward to.

Martin Offiah started the rout after just ten minutes with a remarkable solo try - better than any of the five he scored for the previous day on the same ground for Great Britain. Collecting a loose ball with his back to the line some 40 yards out, he turned, side-stepped and put the gas pedal to the floor to beat John Gallagher's despairing challenge to score in the corner."

The February 28th edition of Doug Laughton's column was headed **"Full steam ahead for the title!".** Referring to the forthcoming home game Sheffield Eagles at the weekend, his column was sub-titled **"We can clip the Eagles wings then go for glory"** Doug wrote:

"We are at the business end of the season. If we had the right result against Hull last night, then we should be in poll position in the title race. We would then need to do the job on the Eagles this Sunday and that would mean we have seven league games left for the run in to the title."

His team got the right result against Hull in a performance Paul Cook described as "stunning". Alan Tait one the players whose form he had called into question in his report on the Wakefield game, scored two fine tries. He had also scored twice in the cup-tie at Barrow. His tries against Hull were set up for him by Tony Myler and Kurt Sorensen respectively - two of the other players Cook stated were not performing their best in the same report. Kurt also helped himself to try in the victory over Hull.

Jonathan Davies made his return to the side for the home game against Sheffield Eagles on March 3rd. He showed his lay-off had not diminished his class and skills by scoring two tries. Despite the return of Davies, it was Widnes who had their wings clipped. The relegation-threatened Yorkshire team came away with a shock 23-14 victory. The Chemics were also dealt a potentially fatal blow in their bid to regain the Championship. They were still two points ahead of Hull and Castleford and five ahead of Wigan. However, the Central Park outfit had three games in hand. One Widnes supporter was so irate about the defeat against Sheffield, that he wrote to the *WWN* criticising Doug Laughton for changing a team that had seemed invincible in the previous six matches. In his weekly column Doug explained that the changes were forced upon him. He highlighted in particular that Tony Myler and Richie Eyres were in hospital, John Devereux had a hamstring problem and that David Hulme had dislocated his thumb.

The loss to Sheffield also did not not bode well for the third round of the Challenge Cup the following Saturday. The Chemics had been drawn away at Warrington, who had been in fine form since defeating them in the Regal Trophy. They did not end hopes of a Challenge Cup triumph at Wembley. Doug Laughton's team were committed and focused and the pack - in particular Esene Faimalo and Emosi Koloto - laid the foundations of an impressive 26-14 victory. Faimalo was different in stature from the gigantic figure of 'The Moose', Less than six feet tall, but with mobility even greater than Koloto and Richie Eyres and perhaps even Phil McKenzie. He was the man-of-the-match at Warrington. He also scored one of two first-half Widnes tries along with David Hulme. The two second-half tries were both scored through interceptions by Andy Currier and Martin Offiah. Martin's effort was from 85 yards out.

There were three league games before the Challenge Cup semi-final. Warrington were beaten again at Naughton Park on the evening of March 20th 25-5. The in-form Andy Currier added another two tries to the one he scored in the Challenge Cup game and Martin Offiah added another one to his try at Wilderspool. On the weekends either side of the home victory against Warrington, Bradford Northern were beaten 32-14 at home and Featherstone Rovers 27-22 away. Having scored two tries on his return to the side in the loss against Sheffield, Jonathan Davies scored tries in all three of the aforementioned victories. He had also resumed goal-kicking duties, which curiously he did not against Sheffield. Although a series of games had been won in style whilst he was sidelined, Davies was the catalyst for the victories over Bradford and Featherstone. He crossed for four tries against Bradford although he only converted two of the seven Widnes scored. Here is how his performance against Bradford was described in the *WWN*:

"There have been few better individual performances than the one turned in by Jonathan Davies on Sunday. Four breath-taking tries ensured that the Chemics title challenge stayed on course, but as well as that they confirmed Davies's stature as one of the game's outstanding attacking players."

WEEKLY NEWS, THURSDAY, MARCH 21, 1991 (Gp

Jonathan just tries and tries

Chemics on course

Widnes 32 pts Bradford Northern 14 pts

THERE can have been few better individual performances by a Widnes player than the one turned in by Jonathan Davies on Sunday.

By PAUL COOK

Bradford threatened to close.

Northern played their part in a hugely

In the win at Featherstone the Chemics had a 27-6 lead and looked to be cruising. With one eye possibly on the forthcoming Challenge Cup semi-final, 16 late points were conceded but they hung on for a vital league victory. Making a two-try debut on the right-wing was Steve Wynn. Like Brimah Kebbie and Ben Eli who also made flying starts to their Widnes careers, Wynn was unable to command a first-team place and only made 18 appearances. Most of his subsequent appearances were at full-back. Despite Wynn's two tries at Featherstone, it was another one scored by Jonathan Davies and one he made for Richie Eyres that were the best of the match. This is how Paul Cook described them in his report:

"Jonathan Davies sparked them into action with a fabulous solo try created out of nothing that saw him split the defence and accelerate away from Pearson as the full-back tried to close. Davies also added the conversion. He then engineered the second try by taking a quick tap when Featherstone anticipated a kick to touch. Racing 70 yards upfield Davies almost scored himself, but when the ball was moved wide Richard Eyres dummied his way over."

In a repeat of the 1989 Challenge Cup semi-final, Widnes were to face St Helens again at Wigan's Central Park ground on Saturday March 30th. In the *WWN* two days before the game, Doug Laughton wrote he had been informed that no Widnes team had beaten St Helens in the Challenge Cup since the 1930 final and the two Widnes half-backs in 1930 were Douglas and Laughton. The headline for Doug's column the following week was **"I FELT LIKE QUITTING."** It told its story of his team's performance. In a throw-back to the previous season's third round defeat against Oldham, again the Chemics never scored a try in an emphatic 2-19 defeat. Martin Offiah and fellow wingman John Devereux were too busy clearing their lines to have any real attacking impact. Jonathan Davies was similarly nullified, and the Hulme brothers at half-back were outplayed.The Saints had a Welsh Jonathan of their own at stand-off who scored two decisive second-half tries Jonathan Griffiths was the man-of-the-match. Kurt Sorensen and Emosi Koloto were overpowered by rival New Zealander George Mann and Great Britain forward Kevin Ward. The headline to Paul Cook's match-report summed the game up in a nutshell: **"Widnes second best all over"** The report began:

"Once again Widnes stumbled within sight of Wembley stadium, but whereas two years they lost the semi-final with dignity and pride intact, here they failed dismally to live up to their reputation. Outfought and outthought by a truly fired up Saints outfit, the Chemics have only themselves for putting up such a poor effort with a place in the final of the game's biggest knock-out competition at stake."

After the Challenge Cup semi-final debacle, it was left to see whether the Chemics could lift themselves to win the Championship. They had three away games at the start of April against the three teams who had beaten them since the turn of the year. They were to face St Helens away just 48 hours after the Challenge Cup semi-final on Easter Monday. Just as they avenged the defeat in the 1989 semi-final, so the 1991 defeat was atoned for with a 22-10. victory. It was strange that the Challenge Cup semi-final was played on an Easter weekend which dictated that the traditional Good Friday fixture against Warrington had to be brought forward. In the programme for the game Doug Laughton in his column headlined **"LEAGUE'S COMPUTER HAS DEVELOPED A BUG!"** wrote

"Well any computer that comes up with a Challenge Cup Semi-Final on a Bank Holiday weekend, depriving clubs of a lucrative Good Friday fixture, has either developed a bug or needs some new software. Tonight's game will be down by possibly 4,000 on a normal Good Friday fixture which has always been a spicy one for the spectators of both clubs."

Widnes were to play Sheffield Eagles away on April 6th. After their shock win at Naughton Park, the Eagles lost their next four games and their battle against relegation from Division One. With the dust settled on the relegation battle, the Chemics needed to win to set up a virtual Championship "decider" at Wigan three nights later and they did, with a hard-earned 18-13 victory There were just two Widnes tries and in contrast to the three scored at St Helens, they were scored by the two main men Jonathan Davies and Martin Offiah. At St Helens two of the three Widnes tries were scored by Steve Wynn and Steve McCurrie who only scored five tries between them in the 1990/91 season. McCurrie played at loose forward at St Helens in place of Les Holliday who was injured in the first-half of the Challenge Cup semi-final.

Everything was set up then for the clash of the big two in British Rugby League. In the previous season's fixture, the Chemics were on a run of six games without a win against a Wigan side that had won their last eight games. Les Holliday inspired them to victory against the odds and a late- season rally that culminated in a third successive Premiership Trophy. The still-injured Holliday would not play this time and Wigan were on an even greater winning streak than in the previous season, one of 15 games. Paul Hulme played at loose-forward and 18-year-old Steve McCurrie was dropped back to the substitutes bench for this make or break game. A crowd of 29,763 packed into Central Park for the encounter.

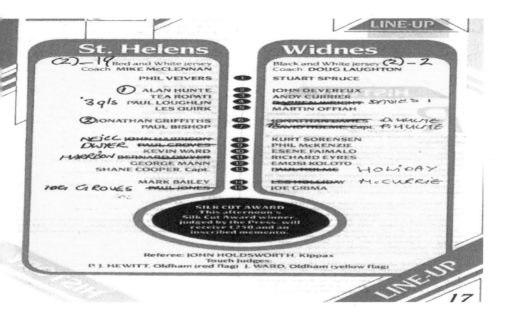

Wigan drew first blood with an early penalty goal by their stand-off half Frano Botica. Botica, a signing from South African Rugby Union, was possibly the deadliest and most accurate goalkicker in the game's history, although he failed to convert a try he scored late in the first-half. Prior to his try, Widnes had cancelled out his early penalty with a superb converted try. In the 12th minute, John Deveruax made a typical powerful burst from inside the Widnes half before passing to fellow Welshman Jonathan Davies who raced under the posts. Another penalty goal by Botica and then his unconverted try gave Wigan a narrow 8-6 interval lead. The Chemics never really threatened in the second-half. As the momentum was with Widnes in the "decider" two years earlier at Naughton Park, with home advantage and perhaps destiny on their side, this time it was with Wigan. They scored three more converted tries to win 26-6.

Wigan had put one hand on the Championship Trophy. They were now top of Division One for the first time in the 1990/91 season. A point clear and with a game in hand, one win from their two remaining games and the Championship was won. They were to play Bradford Northern at Central Park two nights later. There had been some controversy regarding the date of the Wigan-Widnes encounter. Wigan were scheduled to play Bradford on Tuesday April 9th and the Chemics two nights later. Apparently, Wigan chairman Maurice Lindsay persuaded the Rugby League authorities to reverse the dates. Even so, Wigan I think deserved their 1990/91 Championship success. They had really raised the bar under Australian coach John Monie. Doug Laughton's team had only lost six league games - the same as when they won the 1987/88 Championship - but it was not enough in the 1990/91 season. Even if they had not lost to Sheffield at home in March, they may still have lost the Championship on points difference. More crucial than the loss to Sheffield, was the fact that they lost their two league games against Wigan.

With the Championship lost, Widnes did not extend themselves as they defeated relegated Rochdale Hornets in the last league game of the season 44-20 at Naughton Park. They were perhaps saving themselves for an assault on a fourth successive Premiership Trophy. In the first round on April 21st, the Chemics flexed their muscles and showed that they meant Premiership Trophy business by thrashing Bradford Northern 46-18. In the previous week's stroll against Rochdale they had scored eight tries. Remarkably, all eight were scored by different players. Against Bradford they scored nine and three-quarters John Devereux, Darren Wright and Jonathan Davies all scored twice. Davies also kicked five goals to break the Club's points-scoring record for a season. Catching the eye of Paul Cook however, was stand-off half Barry Dowd. The headline of his match-report was **"DOWD'S THE NAME."** The report began:

"While the national newspaper headlines picked up on Jonathan Davies record-breaking performance as the main story of the match, the most significant contribution came from another quarter. Davies may have garnered the column inches by surpassing Mick Burke's 12-year-old points scoring record, but I think Doug Laughton will have taken greater satisfaction from the performance of stand-off Barry Dowd.

Dowd looked a completely different player from the last couple of occasions he has worn a Widnes shirt when the legacy of a couple of serious injuries looked set to ruin his career. Moving closer to match fitness, Dowd seems to hve rediscovered the ureness of touch that once had him earmarked as Tony Myler's natural successor."

Widnes were to contest the semi-final against Featherstone a fortnight ater. Featherstone had beaten Wigan in the first round. The Wigan side may have had their minds on winning the Challenge Cup as in the previous three seasons. They had not contested a Premiership Final since 1987. Martin Offiah was back for he Featherstone game and scored two good tries. Right-winger John Devereux went one bitter and scored a hat-trick, one of which was the try of the match as he powered through from 50 yards. Further tries by Jonathan Davies, Andy Currier and Steve McCurrie added up to an eight-try and 40-point plus haul for the third game in succession. The final score was 42-28, but the Chemics were 42-14 ahead before easing up and conceding 16 late points. A fourth successive Premiership Final had been achieved in great style. The *WWN* reported:

"The Chemics spent an hour of the match playing the kind of outrageously gifted football that sets them apart from most other teams. Then once a fourth successive final was booked, they decided enough was enough. Featherstone took advantage to narrow the gap to 14 points but they were never in with a chance."

Having set the pace for so much of the season in Division One, opponents Hull had fallen away and finished six points behind the Chemics in third place. Widnes were therefore favourites, but on the morning of the game two bombshells hit supporters of the team. It was reported in some national newspapers that Doug Laughton would be leaving the Club to become head-coach at Leeds. If that was not bad enough, it was also reported that Martin Offiah wanted a transfer. Perhaps these were vicious rumours, the timing seemed very strange. The Widnes line up at Old Trafford for the 1991 Premiership Final was:

Alan Tait, John Devereux, Andy Currier, Jonathan Davies, Martin Offiah, Barry Dowd, David Hulme, Kurt Sorensen, Phil McKenzie, Joe Grima, Paul Hulme, Emosi Koloto, Steve McCurrie, Substitutes: Darren Wright and Harvey Howard.

There did indeed seem to be a shadow hanging over the Widnes team in the first-half. A determined and dominant Hull side were 8-0 up at half-time and could have been out of sight. Their Australian coach Noel Cleal who played for Widnes in the 1985/86 season, had reputedly spent 20 hours watching tapes of the present team. I think it's safe to assume he saw a different team on the tapes to the one he was watching from the Old Trafford dug-out. In the second-half the Chemics rallied and got back into the game when the reputedly want-away Offiah scored after David Hulme and Kurt Sorensen split the Hull defence. Jonathan Davies and Alan Tait also had tries disallowed, but Widnes were forcing the issue too late. Ten minutes from time, Hull stand-off and man-of-the-match Greg Mackay created a try for substitute back Gary Nolan which was converted to clinch a 14-4 victory.

The following day it was confirmed that Doug Laughton was to join Leeds and that Martin Offiah wanted a transfer. Doug stated in his book *A Dream Come True* that Leeds made him an offer he could not refuse. Was the disappointment of the Challenge Cup semi-final defeat and the narrow loss of the Championship a factor in Doug's decision also? As already written, he did state that he almost quit after the Challenge Cup semi-final. His departure from the Club was the front-page story of the May 16th edition of the *WWN*. Martin Offiah has certainly highlighted the defeat against St Helens as one of the reasons he wanted a transfer. I think Doug's departure was a factor also. There was a close bond between the two men. Martin dedicated his autobiography to his parents, brother and sister and to Doug. In *A Dream Come True* Doug referred to Martin as "a son". Martin Offiah was never to play for Widnes again. Doug also stated in his book that had he have stayed at Widnes, Martin may have done also.

It was a sad, even tragic end to a season that had promised so much. Doug's team had begun the season by defeating Wigan twice. At Christmas although running neck and neck with Hull in the Championship race, they were five point clear of Wigan. Doug had intimated that his team could "win the lot". Though his team lost the Rrgal Trophy semi-final to Warrington, a Championship, Challenge Cup and Premiership Trophy treble looked possible even in March. Particularly after the 38-0 massacre of Leeds at Headingley. The headline for Paul Cook' match-report was **"End Of An Era?"**. His report began:

"It might be too soon to be talking about Sunday's defeat in terms of the end of an era, but it was somewhat appropriate that Widnes should go down amid the rumour surrounding this Premiership final. Five seasons ago it was a Premiership first round against Wigan that gave the first inkling that Widnes might be on the verge of something big. After a disappointing season they took the champions all the way in a stirring game at Central Park which showed that Widnes might just be able to live with the best.

That summer Doug Laughton added Martin Offiah to his blossoming young squad and the stage was set for Widnes to become the game's most exciting attacking outfit. The mood after that Premiership tie was one of optimism, after Sunday's fourth successive final it was more of bitterness and outrage. Talk of Offiah and Laughton on the move clouded the game on the pitch. Hull deserved their victory but Doug Laughton convinced no-one when he said that the stories surrounding his and Offiah's departure had not affected the Chemics performance."

One player whose performance was not affected at Old Trafford was of course Kurt Sorensen. No matter whether he was captain or not or what was happening on or off the field, he gave the same 200 percent performance and led from the front, Paul Cook reported that Kurt "ran himself into the ground." against Hull. Cook also said the same about Joe Grima, and also praised the performances of Paul Hulme and the emerging Steve McCurrie. It was the performances of Sorensen and Paul Hulme in particular that answered Cook's question as to whether it was the end of an era or not. Kurt's career was not to finish at the end of the 1990/91 season after all. He had unfinished business, not at the *Top of the Town*, but at Wembley Stadium. Whilst he was still around any Widnes team would still be formidable. Paul Hulme along with David Hulme was one of the foundations on which Doug Laughton had built a brilliant Widnes team. And as David had stated early in the season, even without Martin Offiah Widnes still had a lot of speed and talent in the side. The house that Doug built was not ready to fall just yet.

Of course, any team losing Martin Offiah was going to be diminished and equally any team signing him would be enhanced. Martin was to sign for Wigan in January 1992. His signing gave them the advantage over the team who had stopped their complete dominance of British Rugby League in the last four seasons. However, in the 1991/92 season even without the great wingman, Widnes would win a major trophy in brilliant style. The performance in the final was so good that Widnes fans were roaring "are you watching Offiah!" in the second-half.

And there may have been a grimace on the face of the man who brought Martin to Widnes.

DOUG'S FINAL STRAW

Leeds swoop after Premiership flop...

By Denis Lancaster

DOUG Laughton's second stint as coach at Widnes Rugby League club came to an end on Monday.

It was announced he would take over at Leeds next month.

The Headingley club's revelation was confirmed by Widnes 24-hours later in a terse statement issued by General Manager John Stringer on behalf of the committee.

It read: "We have written to Leeds, deploring their unprofessional conduct in approaching Mr Laughton when he was still under contract and without permission. We are sorry he has left us - we made every effort to keep him."

Laughton said: "I have simply got as far as I could ..... with Widnes and the time was right.

Fixtures, results, attendances and points scorers 1990/91 season

Opposition	Venue	Result	Attend.	Goals	Tries
AUGUST					
19 Wigan (Charity Shield)	Swansea	24- 8	11,187	Davies (2)	Davies (3), Devereux, Offiah
26 Whitehaven (Lancashire Cup 1)	Away	70- 6	4,054	Davies (9)	Davies (4), Offiah (3), Tait (2) D. Hulme, Wright, Currier, Myler
SEPTEMBER					
2 Wigan (Lancashire Cup 1)	Home	**24-22**	13,686	**Davies (6)**	**Davies, Offiah, Devereux**
9 Bradford Northern	Away	14-10	6,791	Davies (3)	Wright (2)
12 Warrington (Lancashire Cup 2)	Home	**20- 4**	11,708	**Davies (4)**	**Myler, Wright, Tait**
16 Featherstone Rovers	Home	**41-14**	6,566	**Davies (6), McCurrie dg**	**Devereux (2), A. Eyres (2), Currier, Wright, Ashurst**
23 Hull	Away	6-32	7,712	Davies	Tait
29 Salford (Lancashire Cup Final)	Wigan	24-18	7,485	Davies (4)	Currier, Myler, Smith, Offiah
OCTOBER					
2 Oldham	Home	**24-16**	7,631	**Davies (4)**	**Devereux, Currier, Tait, Offiah**
6 Castleford	Home	**46- 4**	4,185	**Davies (5)**	**Offiah (3), D Hulme (2), Myler, Currier, McKenzie, Holliday**
14 Hull Kingston Rovers	Away	20-22	6,203	Davies (2)	Myler (2), Davies, Devereux
21 Wakefield Trinity	Away	16- 6	5,530	Davies (2)	Davies (2), Koloto
NOVEMBER					
3 Leeds	Home	**26- 8**	6,163	**Davies (3)**	**Offiah, Devereux, Koloto, D. Hulme, Sorensen**
18 Australia (Tour Game)	Home	**8-15**	14,666	**Davies (2)**	**Davies**
25 Oldham	Away	24-18	5,541	Davies (2)	Davies (2), Wright, Davies, Devereux
DECEMBER					
1 Hull (Regal Trophy 1)	Home	**24-16**	4,940	**Davies (2)**	**Devereux (2), Davies, Offiah, D. Hulme**
8 Leeds (Regal Trophy 2).	Home	**22- 6**	3,465	**Davies (3)**	**Currier (2), D. Hulme, Offiah**
16 Batley (Regal Trophy 3)	Home	**56- 6**	6,665	**Davies (6)**	**Offiah (4), Currier (3), Davies, Atcheson, Faimalo, Tait**
19 Hull Kingston Rovers	Home	**28- 8**	5,344	**Davies (4)**	**Offiah (4), Currier**
26 Warrington	Away	6- 2	8,401	Currier	D. Hulme
29 Warrington (Regal Trophy semi)	Wigan	4- 8	7,478		Offiah
JANUARY					
1 St Helens	Home	**14- 8**	10,494	**Devereux**	**Offiah, Smith, Devereux**
6 Castleford	Away	10-20	6,212	Holliday	R. Eyres (2)
19 Wigan	Home	**14-22**	7,365	**Holliday**	**Offiah (2), Spruce**
30 Rochdale Hornets	Away	60- 6	2,836	Currier (8)	R .Eyres (3), Lia (2) Devereux (2), Currier, Faimalo, Tait, D. Hulme
FEBRUARY					
3 Wakefield Trinity	Home	**34- 6**	6,300	**Currier (3)**	**Offiah (3), McKenzie, Devereux, D. Hulme, Spruce**
10 Doncaster (Challenge Cup 1)	Away	30- 4	5,000	Currier (3), Devereux (2)	Devereux (2), Currier, Tait, McKenzie
17 Leeds	Away	38- 0	12,313	Currier (5)	Currier (3), Offiah, Grima, Spruce, Devereux
24 Barrow (Challenge Cup 2)	Away	28- 4	4,155	Currier (2)	Offiah (2), Tait (2), D. Hulme, R. Eyres
27 Hull	Home	**28- 2**	8,404	**Currier (4)**	**Tait (2), Devereux, Offiah, Sorensen**
MARCH					
3 Sheffield Eagles	Home	**14-23**	6,014	**Currier**	**Davies (2), McKenzie**
9 Warrington (Challenge Cup 3)	Away	26-14	8,638	Davies (5)	D. Hulme, Koloto, Currier, Offiah
17 Bradford Northern	Home	**32-14**	7,282	**Davies (2)**	**Davies (4), Wright, D. Hulme, Offiah**
20 Warrington	Home	**25- 6**	8,166	**Davies (4) dg**	**Currier (2), Davies, Offiah**
24 Featherstone Rovers	Away	27-22	5,247	Davies (3) dg	Wynne (2), Davies, R. Eyres, Koloto
30 St Helens (Challenge Cup semi)	Wigan	2-19	16,109	Davies	
APRIL					
1 St Helens	Away	20-12	7,301	Davies (4)	McCurrie, D. Hulme, Wynne
6 Sheffield Eagles	Away	18-13	3,500	Davies (5)	Davies, Offiah
9 Wigan	Away	6-26	29,763	Davies	Davies
14 Rochdale Hornets	Home	**44-20**	4,634	**Davies (6)**	**Davies, D. Hulme, P. Hulme, McKenzie, Koloto, Offiah, Devereux, Currier**
21 Bradford Northern (Premiership 1)	Home	**46-10**	5,419	**Davies (5)**	**Davies (2), Currier (2), Wright (2), Devereux, McKenzie, Koloto**
MAY					
5 Featherstone Rovers (Premiership 2)	Home	**42-28**	8,358	**Davies (4), Currier**	**Devereux (3), Offiah (2), Davies, McCurrie, Currier**
12 Hull (Premiership Final)	Manchester	4-14	42,043		Offiah

Players total number of games and points 1990/91 season

	Played	Goals	Tries	Points
Chris Ashurst	12		1	4
Paul Atcheson	3		1	4
Jason Critchley	3			0
Andy Currier	41	28	23	148
Paul Davidson	3			0
Jonathan Davies	34	(2dg) 110	30	342
John Devereux	37	2	23	96
Barry Dowd	8			0
Andy Eyres	1		2	8
Richie Eyres	34		7	28
Esene Faimalo	24		2	8
Joe Grima	39		1	4
Les Holliday	24	2	1	8
Harvey Howard	11			0
David Hulme	39		14	56
Paul Hulme	30		1	4
Emosi Koloto	38		6	24
Ben Lia	2		2	8
Steve McCurrie	13	(1dg)	2	9
Phil McKenzie	41		6	24
Paul Moriarty	3			0
Tony Myler	28		6	24
Martin Offiah	37		41	164
David Smith	10		2	8
Kurt Sorensen	34		2	8
Alan Tait	28		12	48
Darren Wright	32		9	36
Steve Wynne	5		3	12

First Division	Games	Won	Drawn	Lost	For	Against	Points
Wigan	26	20	2	4	652	313	42
Widnes	**26**	**20**	**0**	**6**	**635**	**340**	**40**
Hull	26	17	0	9	513	367	34
Castleford	26	17	0	9	578	442	34
Leeds	26	14	2	10	602	448	30
St Helens	26	14	1	11	628	553	29
Bradford Northern	26	13	1	12	434	492	27
Featherstone Rovers	26	12	1	13	533	592	25
Warrington	26	10	2	14	404	436	22
Wakefield Trinity	26	10	2	14	356	409	22
Hull Kingston Rovers	26	9	3	14	452	615	21
Oldham	26	10	0	16	481	562	20
Sheffield Eagles	26	7	2	17	459	583	16
Rochdale Hornets	26	1	0	25	317	912	2

6) 1991/92 season "Are you watching Offiah!"

Club legend Frank Myler was re-appointed as first-team coach for the 1991/92 season. Frank had previously held the position between 1975 and 1978, when ironically, he was succeeded by the man he was now replacing. It was his first coaching post since leaving Oldham in 1987 with whom he had been with for seven years. During his time at Oldham, he was also head of the Great Britain team that toured Australia in 1984. As in 1975, he was inheriting a talented group of players. In 1975 the team Frank took over was on the rise, having won their first major trophies in over a decade. In 1992 he was taking over a team which Doug Laughton had intimated he could not take any further. Frank also had contractual problems with some players to sort out, and had to deal with the want-away Martin Offiah. To compound these issues the Club lost another £112,000 as average attendances dropped by another 1,000 a game during the 1990/91 season.

On the playing side, Frank's reign got off on the wrong foot. The loss to St Helens in the pre-season friendly was inconsequential, as Widnes had not won it during Doug's second spell at the helm. The 18-27 away defeat to Second Division Workington Town in the Lancashire Cup was a different matter, and did not bode well for the season ahead. The week after their Lancashire Cup exit, the Chemics commenced their league fixtures at Naughton Park on the first day of September. Doug Laughton had commented the previous season about the league computer scheduling a Challenge Cup semi-final on an Easter weekend. Perhaps he thought it had gone haywire again, by scheduling his first game as Leeds coach at the ground of the club he had left.

The Leeds hierarchy obviously thought Doug was the man to arrest years of under-achievement. Leeds had never won the Championship in over 20 years and not appeared in a Challenge Cup Final since 1978. Doug's rapid return to where he had instigated so much achievement in that period, did the attendance no harm whatsoever. On a perfect day for playing rugby, a crowd of 10,666 watched the game and the Widnes team shrugged off the defeat at Workington with a narrow but satisfying 12-10 victory. The Chemics wore for the first time at Naughton Park a new kit. A modification on the predominantly white top and black shorts, there were two black and one red bands on the front of the shirt. Oddly, the jersey was introduced in the previous season's Premiership Final defeat against Hull.

The first away league game of the season was at Wigan of all places on September 8th. Widnes did not repeat their victory over Leeds, but gave an encouraging performance. They went toe-to-toe with the Wigan side before going down 18-28. They equalled the four tries scored by the Champions, but the deadly goal-kicking of Frano Botica made the difference. He punished the Chemics heavily for conceding needless penalties. The form of John Devereux and captain Tony Myler in the first two league games was particularly good. "Devs" who had scored a try against Leeds, scored again at Wigan after taking a typical long Myler pass. His fellow Welshman Jonathan Davies also scored after taking a clever reverse pass from Tony. Myler who had outplayed his international rival Gary Scholfield in the Leeds game, also scored a try himself at Wigan. The Maestro was in his 12th season at Widnes, but his genius and skills seemed undiminished. His performance at Wigan prompted Paul Cook to write in the *WWN* match-report:

"Tony Myler was easily Widnes's stand-out player and didn't deserve to be on the losing side. For the full eighty minutes he was in the thick of the action and you just have to pray that the gifted stand-off will last a full season."

It was appropriate that there was a picture of Tony on the front of the match-day programme for the third league game of the season on September 28th. He scored another try as the Chemics defeated Hull Kingston Rovers 24-6 at Naughton Park. Phll McKenzie made a typical sniping run before passing to him, and he showed his strength to force his way over the try-line. Myler was also involved in a passing movement with Alan Tait which led to another Jonathan Davies try. Given that Tony had shown Mr Schofield who was the boss in the opening game against Leeds, one wonders if he had been selected for 1990 Ashes series, a narrow series loss might have been a victory. His early-season form was tremendous. Unfortunately, Paul Cook's prayer that he would last a full season was not answered. Tony was to have an operation on a neck injury which was to keep him sidelined until February 1992.

The Chemics finished their September fixtures with an 18-10 victory at Salford. Paul Cook in his match-reports was not as impressed with the defeats of Hull K.R. and Salford as he was with the performances against Leeds and Wigan. Even so, three wins out of four with the only defeat being at Wigan, was not a bad start to the second Frank Myler regime at all. As Doug Laughton had a weekly column in the *WWN*, so too did Frank. The week following the Salford game Frank's column was headlined **"You ain't seen nothin yet!"** Frank began:

"Well the season has got underway in earnest now, and with three wins out of four under our belts I am quietly happy with the way things are going. But as we all know, we have not been playing faultless rugby and we have not been winning with a great deal of style which we are capable of. Sunday's game at Salford was a typical example of how we have performed so far."

FIRST TEAM SQUAD BEFORE THE START OF THE 1991/2 SEASON

BACK ROW: FROM LEFT TO RIGHT: Harvey Howard, David Smith, Les Holliday, Joe Grima, Andy Currier, Chris Ashurst.
MIDDLE: Mark Sarsfield, John Devereux, Barry Dowd, Paul Moriarty, Richie Eyres, Darren Wright, Stuart Spruce, Kurt Sorensen.
FRONT: Paul Hulme, Steve McCurrie, David Hulme, Tony Myler, Phil McKenzie, Alan Tait.

The proclamation of the headline seemed to be fulfilled during the month of October. His team won their next three league games and went to the top of Division One. The first victory was a narrow away win at Castleford on October 6th. The 22-20 victory was similar in scoreline and manner to a couple at the Wheldon Road ground during the Laughton era. Paul Cook praised the resolution of the Widnes team who were eight points behind at the break. Swinton and Featherstone Rovers were beaten in a more comfortable manner at Naughton Park the following weekends 44-12 and 34-20 respectively.

Scoring tries in all three victories were John Devereux and Darren Wright. Devereux scored a brace in the two home games, and Wright scored a hat-trick against Featherstone. Amongst the try-scorers also in the two successive home games was New Zealand forward Te "Tiny" Solamona. Signed by Frank Myler at the start of the season, he had made his debut at Castleford. His promising start did not last, and he only played 14 first-team games and scored no further tries. Playing his only full first-team game against Featherstone was former St Helens scrum-half Neil Holding. He had been signed on a month-long loan deal in exchange for Joe Grima from Oldham, to where Solamona was eventually transferred. The Chemics last fixture in October was a preliminary tie in the Regal Trophy away to relegated Rochdale Hornets. In contrast to the 60-6 massacre at Rochdale the previous season. Frank Myler's team were made to work hard for their 24-14 victory.

On the playing front at least, the fortunes of the Club were going well without the departed Doug Laughton and the absent Martin Offiah. The run of victories in October seemed to vindicate a feature in the September 19th edition of the *WWN* that gave the opinion that the Club should sell Offiah. The feature divided opinion amongst supporters who corresponded the following week. Sadly, there were some whose anger with Martin's continued absence went too far. On the front-page of the October 24th edition it was reported that he had received hate mail. On the back-page it was reported that Jonathan Davies had been given a new three-year contract. If this was good news to some supporters, it may have been doused by a report also that Alan Tait had asked for a transfer. Apparently, the Scottish full-back also wanted his own contract re-newing but was refused.

Already on the transfer-list was Les Holliday, who in contrast to inspiring Widnes to the 1990 Premiership, had finished the previous season injured. He had initially been unable to get a place in Frank Myler's team, but had played his way back into contention. As we shall see, both Tait and Holliday were to remain with the Club for the rest of the season. The fortunes of Les Holliday in particular, were to take a turn for the better The Chemics run of victories was stopped in its tracks in the first fixture of November. They were defeated 28-14 at Halifax in a league game. In his match-report Paul Cook stated:

"It has been common knowledge for some time that without Tony Myler Widnes lack an authoritative midfield playmaker and on Sunday it really showed. David Hulme is not playmaker in the traditional scrum-half sense. Widnes can continue with David Hulme for his other qualities spirit, tenacity and outstanding defence."

Despite criticism of his alleged shortcomings, Hulme scored one of the three Widnes tries. The other two were scored by Welshman John Devereux, who was in a great vein of form. It was the fifth successive game in which he had scored, and he would extend his run for two more games and for another two games in which he actually played. He was averaging over a try a game just as Martin Offiah had done the previous four seasons. His nine-game scoring sequence was second only to Martin's remarkable 15-game sequence at the start of his Widnes career. Martin actually played in the corresponding A-team game against Halifax two nights before the first-team's defeat. Hopes were briefly raised that he would resolve his dispute with the Club. The Chemics bounced back from the Halifax defeat with an emphatic 34-0 hammering of Wakefield Trinity at home on November 10th. Paul Cook sang a different tune than the previous week writing:

"This was far and away Widnes's most convincing performance of the season and the perfect comeback following the defeat at Halifax. Widnes were without Tait, Tony Myler, Sorensen, Koloto and still put on a performance of the highest quality. With Stuart Spruce, Paul Hulme and Steve McCurrie fit again and Joe Grima back from Oldham, the squad strength should be there for Widnes to go on from this to challenge for the game's major honours."

The Chemics did indeed go on from the victory over Wakefield Trinity to put themselves within striking distance of winning the next of the game's major honours. The two remaining fixtures in November and the first game in December, were the first three rounds of the Regal Trophy. Frank Myler's team were given reasonably favourable draws and progressed to the semi-final without too much bother. In the first round they avenged their Lancashire Cup exit by accounting for Workington Town at Naughton Park by 26 points to 8. The following week they travelled to Carlisle to defeat another Second Division team 30-16. In the third round at home to First Division Featherstone Rovers, the game was similar in pattern and scoreline to the league match. The Chemics prevailed 34-22 as against the 34-20 victory in October.

In the 1992/93 season Frank Myler wrote a column in the WWN and home game programmes as Doug Laughton had done. After his team won three of their first four league games he stated "You ain't seen nothin' yet. It is interesting to note what Frank said about "a team which starts with a gallop" given how the season panned out!

Alan Tait showed his attacking panache from the full-back position against Carlisle and Featherstone. Despite his recent transfer request, he scored two tries at Carlisle and one against Featherstone Rovers. Also scoring tries in the two games was left-winger Mark Sarsfield. The Leigh-born academy product for most of the 1991/92 season was to fill the enormous gap left by Martin Offiah. Paul Cook noted that Sarsfield "showed great determination" in scoring at Carlisle. Unfortunately, his early promise and the tries soon dried up. Most of the tries seemed to be coming on the right flank - not a coincidence perhaps with Offiah not playing. The Offiah saga was ongoing and a letter by P. Warner a supporter based in Ormskirk, published in the November 25th edition of the *WWN* accepted the inevitably of Martin leaving the Club, but saw his departure as a "minor hiccup". An article in the sports section of the December 5th edition of the *WWN* was headlined: **"Welsh Wizard goes for 1,000"** The article began:

"Widnes skipper Jonathan Davies needed just 13 points in last night's league game at struggling Bradford Northern for a career total of 1,000."

Obviously written before the game at Bradford, the article seemed to imply the formality of Widnes defeating a team with just one league victory since the start of the season. Jonathan may have reached the milestone at Bradford had he played on the right-wing as he had done early in his Widnes career. Steve Wynn playing in the position scored three tries of which Davies converted one. They were the only Widnes points scored as the form-book was turned upside down. The Chemics slumped to their third league defeat of the season. The hefty 14-36 loss was untimely with Wigan to play at home next. Wigan had incurred some shock defeats themselves since the start of the season. They had lost four league games and were knocked out of the Lancashire Cup and Regal Trophy. They beat Widnes despite the sending-off of scrum-half Andy Gregory before half-time. The final score was almost identical to the previous season, with Widnes again scoring 14 points whilst Wigan scored just one more than the 22 they scored back in February Steve Wynn added to his hat-trick at Bradford by scoring a try from the full-back position. Paul Cook viewed the loss as an opportunity missed writing:

"Losing to Wigan is always difficult to swallow. It is even harder to accept when they are not quite firing on all cylinders and Widnes can't take advantage."

Steve Wynn was back on the right-wing for the next league game at Wakefield on December 15th. With so many Widnes tries being scored on the right-wing in the 1991/92 season, it seemed inevitable he would score again and he did. Mark Sarsfield scored his third and last try of the season playing on the left-wing. The tries by the two wingmen at Wakefield gave the Chemics an 8-0 lead and they seemed to be on course for victory. Unfortunately, fog descended and the game had to be abandoned. In the December 12th edition of the *WWN* Frank Myler voiced his frustration at the fog throwing a spanner in the works of a potential Widnes victory. In the same edition of the *WWN* it was reported that forward Paul Moriarty was out for the rest of the season. It was wretched luck for the Welshman who had been establishing himself in Frank Myler's team after playing only three games the previous season because of injury. Indeed, Paul Cook reporting on the Wigan game highlighted the absence of Moriarty and Koloto as the reason why the Wigan forwards dominated.

The semi-final of the Regal Trophy against St Helens was to be contested on Saturday, December 21st at Central Park, Wigan. The Challenge Cup semi-final defeats against the Saints in 1989 and earlier in the year, were perhaps still on the minds of both players and supporters. The conditions were foul, but a combination of strong winds and rain did not stop a vintage first-half performance that ensured an 18-10 Widnes victory. In the first 12 minutes the Chemics scored at a point a minute with two superb converted tried by centres Andy Currier and Darren Wright. On the half-hour mark, the mobile Esene Faimalo scored a third try and Jonathan Davies should have been awarded a further obstruction try. Paul Cook's match-report in the *WWN* began:

"Widnes handed their supporters the best possible Christmas present as they battled to reach a record eighth Regal Trophy final. The Black and Whites put on a dazzling display in the first 40 minutes and then battened down the hatches when it looked as if Saints were about to stage a remarkable come-back. Widnes richly deserved the chance to take on Leeds in the final after coming through a titanic struggle that should have made exciting rugby virtually impossible.

Everywhere you looked there was a man-of-the-match candidate and Alan Tait's powerful running from full-back just earned him the official nomination. But there would have no complaints had the award gone to Les Holliday, either of the Hulme brothers or Andy Currier. In the first half Saints were simply blown away by the strength of the Widnes challenge. With Koloto and Sorensen providing the lead, the mid-field challenges on men like Ward, Mann and Forber stopped Saints getting to grips with the game."

WIDNES handed their supporters the best possible Christmas present as they battled to reach a record eighth Regal Trophy final.

Widnes 18 St Helens 10
By PAUL COOK

The Black and Whites put on a dazzling display in the first 40 minutes and then battened down the hatches when it looked as if Saints were about to stage a remarkable come-back.

But there would have been no complaints had the award gone to Les Holliday, either of the Hulme brothers or Andy Currier.

In the first half Saints were simply blown away by the strength of the Widnes challenge. With Koloto and Sorensen providing the lead, the mid-field challenges on men like Ward, Mann and Forber stopped Saints getting to grips with the game.

again much in evidence for the second score. Holliday threw out a lovely short ball to Tait whose pace and strength took him out of one tackle and into the clear. He drew the remaining cover before handing on to Currier who shot over unopposed. Davies drove the conversion against the crossbar.

Saints were shellshocked by this start and hardly made a decent break while Widnes looked ready to do some damage whenever they got the chance to use the ball.

The third try came on the half-hour when Holliday found Esene Faimalo racing up in support and the powerful prop brushed aside Shane Cooper's

End of an Era

The Chemics finished 1991 defeating Warrington at home on Boxing Day by 20 points to 8. All the points scored by both teams came by the way of unconverted tries. The visitors were down to 12 men from early in the second-half. Even so, it was a good Widnes performance with the returning John Devereux scoring twice and Richie Eyres who also scored, being the outstanding players. The match-programme featured tributes to the father of Andy Currier who had been tragically killed in a recent accident and Warrington's legendary Australian wingman Brian Bevan who died earlier in 1991. It had been a year since Doug Laughton had suggested his Widnes team could win everything in the 1990/91 season. That dream was shattered when they lost to Warrington almost immediately in the Regal Trophy semi-final. Under Frank Myler's regime a Regal Trophy Final place was already assured. With the team just a point behind Doug's Leeds team at the top of Division One, the vibe of winning everything must have again been prevalent. Indeed, the headline of Paul Cook's match-report in the *WWN* was **"Title comes a touch closer** which began:

"Widnes fans have had plenty to enthuse about over Christmas - first a Regal Trophy final place then this convincing victory over title rivals Warrington. Admittingly, it took the dismissal of Wire half-back Kevin Ellis to turn the tide Widnes's way, but once they had the advantage there was no danger of them letting it slip. Eyres scored a much-deserved try for another afternoon's non-stop endeavour and John Devereux signalled his return to action with another brace of tries."

The Championship which Paul Cook intimated may have been a step closer after beating Warrington on Boxing Day, was suddenly a few steps away in the first week of the new year. They incurred two bad defeats at St Helens on New Year's Day and at home to Castleford on January 5th. They were bad defeats for different reasons. Against Warrington on Boxing Day, Widnes played against 12 men from early in the second-half. At St Helens they faced 12 from the fourth minute of the game when Saints forward George Mann was sent off for a high tackle on Esene Faimalo. Jonathan Davies slotted over the resulting penalty, but it was the only Widnes goal of the game. They again scored five unconverted tries including another couple by John Devereux. A one-man advantage and 14-2 lead after 22 minutes play were squandered. A St Helens try in the last five minutes gave them a 24-22 victory. In the home defeat against Castleford, Widnes simply played poorly. scoring just one unconverted try. Even free-scoring John Devereux had a bad afternoon. Not only did his nine game try-scoring sequence end, but he was beaten to a loose ball by opposing winger David Nelson three minutes from time who wrapped up a 14-4 Castleford victory.

The two defeats against St Helens and Castleford did not bode well for the forthcoming Regal Trophy Final against Leeds at Central Park, Wigan. Doug Laughton seemed to be working his magic as Leeds coach. His team were on a run of 10 successive victories, top of the First Division, and understandably favourites to defeat the Chemics. One of the few trophies the Leeds Club had won in the previous decade and more was in 1984, when they defeated Widnes in the final of the then John Player Trophy. A repeat victory was expected to kick-start an era of success under the stewardship of Doug. In order to achieve this, he had signed Widnes-born half-back prodigy Bobby Goulding from Wigan. To add experience, he had also signed Mike O'Neill, whom he had sold to Rochdale after the 1990 Premiership Final. Doug's prize coup was signing the great Ellery Hanley from Wigan early in the season. Hanley was injured and not in the Leeds line-up.

Though Joe Grima was back from his loan spell at Oldham, Widnes had worse injury problems. Esene Faimalo, Emosi Koloto, Paul Moriarty, all of whom were Frank Myler's first-choice forwards, were unfit to play. David Hulme who had not played since the Boxing Day victory over Warrington, was also missing from the Widnes team. Paul Hulme was at hooker in place of Phil McKenzie and had been for the last few games. Barry Dowd was a surprise selection at scrum-half. It was though the non-selection of McKenzie that surprised BBC co-commentator Wigan coach John Monie the most. On a cold, misty afternoon a crowd of 15,023 attended the 1992 Regal Trophy Final. The Widnes line-up was:

Alan Tait, John Devereux, Andy Currier, Darren Wright, Mark Sarsfield, Johathan Davies, Barry Dowd, Kurt Sorensen, Paul Hulme, David Smith, Harvey Howard, Richie Eyres, Les Holliday. Substitutes Paul Atcheson and Joe Grima.

In the opening exchanges Widnes looked out of sorts, but soon hit their stride and took a grip on the game. After 10 minutes Andy Currier was held up over the Leeds try-line after a run from the acting half-back position. Jonathan Davies missed a penalty, before a Les Holliday drop-goal put the Chemics in front. They needed a try to reflect their superiority as the half-hour mark approached. A couple of efforts were disallowed. First, Currier popped up on the left-side of the field and put left-winger Mark Sarsfield in at the corner, but the pass was judged to be forward. From the ensuing scrum, Widnes won the ball against the head. In the following passag of play, Alan Tait got over the line but was judged to have been held up as Andy Currier had been.

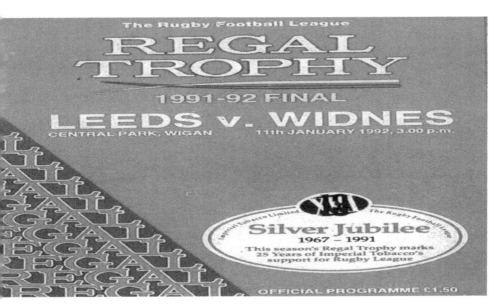

Five minutes later, the Chemics got the break through and scored the first of four thrilling tries. Inside his own half, Les Holliday chipped the ball over the Leeds defence and caught it on the full. He transferred the ball on to Darren Wright, who raced 25 yards before handing on to the supporting Jonathan Davies who finished the sweeping 60-yard move off. The Welshman converted to give his team a team a 7-0 interval lead.

Early in the second-half Davies, now finding his kicking range, slotted over another penalty to stretch the lead to 9-0. A two-try scoring burst midway through the second-half put the final nails into the Leeds coffin. Man-of-the-match Les Holliday hoisted a huge "bomb" into the Wigan air 25 yards from the Leeds line. The kick bamboozled everybody except himself, he followed up and claimed the rolling ball to score another converted try. Barely three minutes later, Holliday sent John Devereux powering down the right-wing. Alan Tait raced up in support of his Welsh team-mate. Seeing that a Leeds defender was between himself and the Scotsman, "Devs" kicked ahead and this time Tait was not denied, as he followed up to score an unconverted try. The victory was turning into a rout and jubilant Widnes fans were now heard chanting "Are you watching Offiah!" Jonathan Davies dropped another goal to round the score to 20-0. and the icing on the Widnes cake came seven minutes from time. Joe Grima on as substitute for Les Holliday, carried on from where Holliday had left off. He bust open the Leeds defence on the half-way line raced forward 25 yards before passing to Kurt Sorensen. The King romped the next 25 yards to score a deserved try. Kurt had given a storming performance - then again so had every single Widnes player.

There were jubilant scenes at the end of the match as the players were mobbed by ecstatic Widnes fans. It was if the 24-0 triumph had clinched the Championship or the Challenge Cup. The pre-match mood which was perhaps downbeat after two defeats and the sale of Martin Offiah to Wigan, had completely evaporated. Offiah's £440,000 transfer to Wigan had been given extensive coverage in the January 9th edition of the WWN. In addition to the transfer being covered on the front and back pages, an editorial opinion was also published. The forthcoming Regal Trophy Final almost seemed peripheral. The January 16th edition was completely different and the sub-headline on the front-page was **"Widnes march on to Regal Trophy victory."** There was also a picture of man-of-the-match Les Holliday in addition to the sub-headline. Paul Cook wrote in his match-report:

"What a victory this was! A victory that oozed class, that was filled with consummate professionalism and that re-established Widnes as more than just a force to reckoned with. Widnes didn't just end Leeds hopes of a first major trophy in eight years, they systematically tore them apart and sounded a warning to anyone prepared to write them off that there's plenty more to come. An era ended when Doug Laughton and Martin Offiah declared their intentions to leave.

But Frank Myler has stepped in and left his own indelible stamp on another generation of Black and White stars. The cavalier years of Laughton's reign may be gone for good, but there was a passion about Widnes's play on Saturday that was rarely seen last season. The foundations for victory were laid in the pack where all six had mighty games. Les Holliday shaded the man-of-the-match award from veteran Kurt Sorensen but those two experienced hands would the first to pay tribute to the likes of David Smith and Harvey Howard who flourished on the big stage."

After the Lord Mayor's show in the Regal Trophy Final, the prospect of getting back into the Championship race and winning the Challenge Cup seemed bright. Certainly, Frank Myler intimated as much both in the *WWN*, and in the match-programme for the next league game at home to Hull on January 19th. His team narrowly defeated the Humberside team to keep their Championship hopes alive. John Devereux put them on the way to a 14-0 interval lead with a great try in which he beat four defenders. Perhaps the Chemics eased off, as they were to face the St Helens at home in the first round of the Challenge Cup the following week. They eventually scraped a 22-20 win after some scares in the second-half. It was timely that Jonathan Davies had re-gained his goal-kicking form. He kicked five to secure the vital victory for the Chemics as the Devereux try was only one of three scored against Hull's four.

In the next two games it was not another goal, but a try-scoring drought that was experienced. And any hopes of adding the Championship or Challenge Cup to the Regal Trophy were abruptly ended. In the Challenge Cup game on February 1st, St Helens put Widnes out of the competition yet again. Just as in the previous season's semi-final, the Chemics scored just a penalty goal. They played with more passion than in the 1991 semi-final and limited the Saints to 10 points this time around. They did not though show anything like the form they displayed in the Regal Trophy Final or indeed in the semi-final just before Christmas. A letter by supporter Mike White published in the following week's *WWN* partly read:

"The display against St Helens In the first round of the Challenge Cup was bereft of any attacking flair, lacked any effective or imaginative game plan and was delivered by a team who looked incapable of scoring even if Saints had packed up and gone home.

Following their defeats in the 1989 and 1991 Challenge Cup semi-finals by St Helens , the Chemics were beaten again by them in the first round at home in 1992. The *WWN* mistakes the St Helens line-up for the Hull team! In addition, "man-of-the-match" for Widnes, Scottish full-back Alan Tait, is not even in the Chemics line-up!

Mike White's reaction may have been over the top, even so, it was a big disappointment to lose again in the Challenge Cup to St Helens. The headline of Frank Myler's column on February 13th was **"We're not finished yet"** as he focused on the Championship. In the following week's edition, he praised the performances of Alan Tait, John Deveruex, Jonathan Davies, Richie Eyres and Les Holliday, who had all played for a victorious Great Britain team against France the previous week. An article in the Sport section of the *WWN* on February 20th was sub-titled "Stars are fit for the title challenge". The article focused on the five Widnes internationals and their performances against France. The article was obviously written before the previous night's game at Wakefield. The Chemics Championship challenge ended in essence as they again failed to score a try in a 4-12 defeat. Frank Myler must have wished that the game at Wakefield before Christmas when the Chemics were 8-0 up was not abandoned. The defeat in the re-arranged fixture not only ended any Championship hopes, but set the tone for the rest of the season. Two successive victories followed, but it was downhill big-time after that.

The first of the victories whilst impressive in terms of the scoreline was not impressive in terms of performance. Swinton who finished bottom of Division One by a country mile in the 1991/92 season, were beaten away 38-12 on February 23rd. Hooker Phil McKenzie along with Tony Myler, were back in the starting line-up at Swinton. Both were soon out again, Myler with another injury and McKenzie again was out of favour. An 18-8 defeat of Halifax at Naughton Park on the first day in March was again lacklustre. Two players who showed their true class and form in the games were Myler and John Devereux. Back from his early-season injury, Tony played as if he had never been away. It was a feature of his brilliant, but injury-littered career. His class and skills were so good, he never needed a couple of games to get back into his stride as other players did after injury. He also typically laid on a try for the up and coming Stuart Spruce against Halifax.

In the Halifax game Devereux yet again, showed his fire and determination to score a hat-trick of tries. He continued his remarkable form by scoring another three at Leeds the following week. He also kicked four goals as Jonathan Davies was side-lined with injury. Full-back Alan Tait scored the other two Widnes tries as the Chemics rattled up 28 points. They were not though enough to win the game. Doug Laughton's team scored 40 as they gained some revenge for the thrashing they received in the Regal Trophy Final. A month-long rot had set in. The next loss 8-10 at Hull K.R on March 15t was a low-scoring affair in contrast to the game at Leeds. **"What's gone wrong?** " was the headline of the match-report on the 10-17 home defeat to Bradford Northern the following week.

Alarm bells had started ringing as supporters wrote to the *WWN*. Letters were published which were headlined **"We need the will to win"** and **"Get your act together"**. In the same March 26th edition of the *WWN* the headline of Frank Myler's column was: **"I share the fan's disappointment"**. It got even worse the following week, as a will to win and Widnes getting their act together seemed even further away. They were scalped 2-28 at Featherstone in their last fixture in March, and another letter from a "True Supporter" went further than asking "What's gone wrong?", it was assertively and emphatically headlined **"something is wrong"**.

Something was indeed wrong, and the Chemics lost again at home to Salford 20-24 on April 6th despite another two tries from Devereux who had been moved to the right-centre position. The sequence of defeats had sent the Chemics tumbling down the Division One table. An editorial was published in the April 15th editon of he *WWN*. I here reproduce an edited version of that editorial (forgive the pun!):

"Widnes's Rugby League season fell apart when they were knocked out of the RL Cup in the first round. Up to that point, it looked to some extent as though the club would overcome a series of injuries and the unsettling departure of Martin Offiah and its attendant publicity. Defeat in the cup against St Helens was an obvious blow but even worse for the fans has been the cheerless procession of defeats which has left them struggling to qualify for the Premiership play-offs."

One wonders if the editorial was written before the away game at Hull on April 11th. The home team raced into a 10-0 lead and the Chemics looked to be heading for yet another defeat - and perhaps the Second Division! The sequence of defeats had seen them fall from Championship contenders to contenders for relegation. From out of thin air, they conjured up their early-season form and the form that won the Regal Trophy. Belatedly, they responded to Frank Myler's "Buck up!" order which was published in the *WWN* a fortnight earlier. And the catalyst for the vital victory was again John Devereux, who not only scored four tries but kicked four goals. Where would the Chemics have been in the 1991/92 season without the Welshman? **"Devastating Devereux!"** was the headline of Paul Cook's match-report which began:

'About turn' by Chemics
Devastating
Devereux!

WHEN they come to hand out the prizes for the Widnes player of the season, there can only really be one winner.

John Devereux's 24-point haul against Hull only emphasised further his immense value to the team.

He should also be of equal value to Great Britain on tour. If Paul Eastwood has been taken for his durability and kicking prowess, then Devereux is streets ahead of his Hull rival.

When Mal Reilly gets down to the serious business of naming a first choice side Devereux should certainly be in it - either as a centre or winger.

If there has been a better British winger this season - barring Offiah - then I haven't seen him, and in his last two performances in the centre, Devereux has proved to be as good as any in that position as well.

Hull 20   Widnes 36

Widnes: Tait, Critchley, Devereux, Wright, Carbert, Spruce, Dowd, Sorenson, (Grima 63), P Hulme, Howard, Smith, Eyres, Holliday. Sub: McCurrie.
Hull: Gay, Eastwood, G Nolan, Harrison, Turner, McNamara, Mackey, Spring, Jackson, Jones (Wilson 68), Wilson (R Nolan 40), Dunn (Busby 13), Sharp.
Referee: Mr R Smith (Castleford). Attendance: 4,450

Report by PAUL COOK

JOHN DEVEREUX - A 24 point haul

prompted by Les Holliday who looks an altogether happier player when he can find forwards willing to run on to his passes.

In Eyres and Sorenson he had two men ready to do just that and they repeatedly drove the Hull pack backwards.

Before half-time Devereux was twice on the scoresheet for tries and had two goals to his name as Widnes looked to have assumed control.

In the first minute of the second half Richard Gay -Hull's best player - forced his way over for Eastwood to level matters

End of an Era

"When they come to hand out the prizes for the Widnes player of the season there can only really be one winner. John Devereux's 24-point haul only emphasised further his immense value to the team. If there has been a better British winger this season - barring Offiah - then I haven't seen him, and his last two performances in the centre,

Devereux has proved himself to be as good as anyone in that position as well Thankfully he wasn't alone this week in pulling Widnes after they stared a sixth successive defeat in the face. The team, from somewhere suddenly found it within their capability to overcome an early deficit and play some of their best rugby since the turn of the year."

Following the Devereux-inspired victory at Hull, only two remaining league fixtures were to be played. In the traditional Easter fixtures away at Warrington on Good Friday and at home to St Helens on Easter Monday, Widnes got back to "losing ways" to again put a twist on a cliché. The win at Hull however had secured an eighth-place finish in Division One and a place in the Premiership play-off. In the 1991/92 season only two points separated the Chemics and relegated Featherstone Rovers who finished next to the bottom. Featherstone were relegated only on points difference as three other teams finished with 22 points. Yet all four teams finished 16 points clear of bottom of the table Swinton! Although the Chemics lost their two Easter fixtures 8-20 at Warrington and 23-28 to St Helens at Naughton Park, they gave two more encouraging performances.

At Warrington the score was 8-8 late in the game, before mistakes by Les Holliday and Mark Sarsfield gifted the Wires two tries. Holliday threw out a speculative pass that was intercepted by Warrington right-centre Alan Bateman who raced 50 yards to score. Sarsfield missed a loose ball, which was picked up by left-centre Tony Thornfield who also scored. Against St Helens in what transpired to be his last game at Naughton Park, hooker Phil McKenzie scored a brace of first-half tries. Some spectators may have missed his second, which he scored after taking a smart inside pass from Richie Eyres. Their eyes may have been on a brawl between Kurt Sorensen and Saints forward Kieran Dwyer near the touchline! The headline to Paul Cook's match-report was **"In a fighting mood"**. It was not though, alluding to Kurt's fight with Dwyer. It was alluding to the improved form of the Chemics against Hull and in the Easter games and their prospects in the Premiership play-off.

Finishing the season in eighth place in Division One, meant that Widnes were to play Champions Wigan in the first round of the Premiership Trophy play-offs. How the fortunes of the teams had changed since they met at Naughton Park back in December. Wigan's victory in that game was their third in a run of 23. This incredible sequence not only helped them to retain the Championship, but took them to their fifth successive Challenge Cup Final. It was an unbeaten run even longer than in the second-half of the previous season, when they pipped Widnes to the Championship. In contrast, despite their Regal Trophy triumph, the Chemics had lost another 10 leagues games including seven of their last eight. They had also of course, lost in the first round of the Challenge Cup.

The parallels with the 1987 encounter between the two teams in the Premiership play-off were striking. As in 1987, The Wigan team had won the

Championship by a considerable margin. The Widnes team of 1987 had also briefly hovered near the relegation zone. The game was also to be played on exactly the same date April 26th. The Chemics seemed to be on a hiding to nothing as five years earlier. They could only hope that as in the previous four seasons, Wigan may be more focused on winning the Challenge Cup. They had after all, not contested a Premiership Final since 1987. There was a vibe though that Wigan were out to "win the lot" in the 199//92 season. And they now had a certain Martin Offiah in their team to help them add the Premiership Trophy to another Championship and possible Challenge Cup Final victory.

The Champions not only defeated Frank Myler's team, but indeed did go on to win the Premiership Trophy as they did in 1987. They were though as in 1987, given an almighty run for their money by an eighth-placed Widnes team. A possible Widnes upset was denied not by a disallowed try as in 1987, but by a loose pass relatively late in the game. The deadly Frano Botica put Wigan ahead with a penalty goal early on, before Richie Eyres put the Chemics ahead with the first try of the match. The score was level 12-12 as half-time approached. Martin Offiah then finished off a Wigan move which Botica almost inevitably converted.

Botica kicked another penalty just after the interval to give his team an eight-point buffer. But the Chemics were far from finished, and another try was engineered by Les Holliday for left-winger Brian Carbett - a short-term signing from Warrington. Having pulled the score back to 20-16, the Widnes team went for broke. With less than 20 minutes remaining Richie Eyres nearly got over again. They were pressing the Wigan line when a loose pass was picked up by former Widnes star Joe Lydon. Lydon passed out to the star more recently purchased from Widnes.

Jonathan Davies, Les Holliday and John Devereux pictured after the last league game of the season against St Helens at Naughton Park, were the three Widnes players originally selected for the 1992 Great Britain tour of Australia and New Zealand. The Wigan team the Chemics faced in the Premiership Trophy had 10 players selected. Davies was subsequently injured and never toured. Paul Hulme and David Myers replaced injured players during the tour.

There could only be one outcome as Martin Offiah plunged a dagger through the heart of his old team and raced 85 yards to score. The try - and the manner in which it was scored - perhaps understandably demoralised the Chemics. Wigan ran in three more late tries and the final score was 42-16. It was a travesty of a scoreline, and did not reflect how close the game had been for over an hour. Paul Cook accurately began his match-report:

"To use an old but appropriate cliché - this score line does not give a true representation of the game as a whole. Widnes stormed back into the sort of form that should have earned them a top four finish had they played with the same spirit in half the games since the Regal Trophy win.

There were players having storming games all over the park for Widnes. in the pack there was nothing to choose between a Widnes side fielding just one tourist - Les Holliday - and Wigan with a full six on the park. The best prop on display was Harvey Howard while Paul Hulme and Richie Eyres completely outshone Betts and McGinty."

The 1991/92 season had ended sooner than in the previous four seasons. As written in the previously mentioned *WWN* editorial, it perhaps ended after their defeat in the first round of the Challenge Cup. The team seemed to lose focus and purpose after their brilliant Regal Trophy triumph. Perhaps the Martin Offiah saga had a belated, unsettling effect on performances. Frank Myler also commented several times both in the *WWN* and in match-day programmes on injuries. Even so, the Chemics had enough talent and firepower to have finished in the top four at least as Paul Cook implied in his report on the Wigan game. And not just John Devereux, Jonathan Davies and Les Holliday - out of the team and on the transfer-list early in the season - who had all been selected for the Great Britain tour of Australia in the summer of 1992.

Devereux averaged more than a try a game in the 1991/92 season, as Martin Offiah had done in the previous four seasons. What was remarkable about the scoring rate of "Devs" during the season, was that Widnes finished only in eighth place in Division One, and he played some games in the centre. Not to be outdone, over at Wigan Martin averaged two tries a game in the 15 he played before the end of the season. His tally was helped considerably with 10 he scored in a 74-16 massacre of Leeds in the Premiership Trophy semi-final. If Martin had plunged a dagger through the heart of his old team-mates in the first round, he burnt alive at stake his old mentor and his team a fortnight later! Doug Laughton reputedly said after the game "I wish I had left the bugger in London!".

In the 1992/93 season, Widnes did not win any of the game's major honours for the first time since the 1986/87 season. They were never really in the Championship race at any stage in the season. Yet perversely, it was in some respects a more successful season. In contrast to the 1991/92 season, their form in the second-half of the 1992/93 season ensured a top four finish in Division One. They also reached the final of the game's major Cup competition - which some supporters may have regarded as a greater achievement than actually winning the Regal Trophy in 1992. Also, some of the younger players really started to fulfil their potential. Particularly, Stuart Spruce and Harvey Howard. Howard who had storming games in the Regal Trophy Final and in the last game of the season at Wigan, was labelled as "The new Kurt Sorensen" by some Widnes supporters.

It was though the "old" Kurt Sorensen who was to finish the 1992/93 season and his illustrious career at Widnes with a flourish.

So near, yet so far

TO USE an old, but appropriate, cliche - this scoreline doesn't give a true representation of the game as a whole.

Widnes stormed back into the sort of form that should have earned them a top four finish had they played with the same spirit in half the games since the Regal Trophy win.

The game turned, really, on two incidents either side of half-time when Widnes should have had Wigan on the rack.

Sickeningly, Martin Offiah was the man to twist the knife on both occasions and there have been few worse sights in recent seasons than Offiah reaping the acclaim at Central Park in a Wigan shirt, particularly after his second score.

Widnes were again forced to make changes, but in doing so they appear to be coming closer to their ideal line-up.

For an hour they fought the champions tooth and nail and were desperately unlucky to continually find themselves trailing.

There were players having storming games all over the park for Widnes.

Wigan 42 Widnes 16
By PAUL COOK

In the pack there was nothing to choose between a Widnes side fielding one tourist - Les Holliday - and Wigan with a full six on the park.

The best prop on display was Harvey Howard while Paul Hulme and Richie Eyres completely outshone Betts and McGinty.

Flashy

Betts, with a try and one flashy break down the middle of the field when Widnes fell for a Wigan move that always breaks them up, somehow collected man of the match award.

Yet he was left standing in terms of effort and consistent yards gained by both his counterparts in Black and White.

With Les Holliday also having his best game for weeks, Widnes were always going forward with a lot more confidence and with plenty of aggression.

Occasionally there was a little too much in some of the tackles and Widnes's indiscipline in the last 25 minutes was the only black spot on an otherwise gutsy performance.

Widnes started well and after falling behind to an early penalty they notched the opening try of the game when Eyres burst a tackle to stride over.

Widnes started well and after falling behind to an early penalty they notched the opening try of the game when Eyres burst a tackle to stride over.

Five minutes later Betts went through a big gap and had the strength to hold off Spruce as he pushed for the line and Botica converted.

Botica's goals were vital in the long run at keeping Widnes at bay.

Conversion

Widnes struck back when Currier took an inside pass from Sorensen to go over and Devereux's conversion levelled the score at 12-12.

At that point Widnes looked to be flying, but from the kick-off and with only two minutes to go to half-time, they committed a cardinal error.

Holliday lost the ball in the first tackle from the kick off and, three tackles later, Offiah was over in the corner. A magnificent Botica conversion gave Wigan breathing space.

RICHIE EYRES - burst a tackle to stride over and again powered through, only to be caught from behind.

Fixtures, results, attendances and points scorers 1991/92 season

Opposition	Venue	Result	Attend.	Goals	Tries
AUGUST					
25 Workington T(Lancashire Cup 1)	Away	18-27	3,500	Currier (3)	Koloto, Eyres, Spruce
SEPTEMBER					
1 Leeds	Home	**12-10**	**10,666**	**Currier (2)**	**Wright, Devereux**
8 Wigan	Away	18-26	15,901	Davies	Devereux, Davies, Tait, Myler
22 Hull Kingston Rovers	Home	**24- 6**	**5,560**	**Davies (4)**	**Davies, D. Hulme, Myler, Currier**
29 Salford	Away	18-10	4,121	Davies (3)	Davies (2), Faimalo
OCTOBER					
6 Castleford	Away	22-20	6,541	Davies (5)	Davies, Wright, Devereux
13 Swinton	Home	**44-12**	**5,723**	**Davies (8)**	**Devereux (2), Davies, Solomona, D. Hulme, Wright, Eyres**
20 Featherstone Rovers	Home	**34-20**	**5,400**	**Davies (5)**	**Wright (3), Devereux (2), Solomona**
29 Rochdale Hornets (Regal Trophy preliminary)	Away	24-14	2,345	Davies (2)	Dowd, Currier, Davies, Tait, Devereux
NOVEMBER					
3 Halifax	Away	14-28	7,429	Currier (2)	Devereux (2), D. Hulme
10 Wakefield Trinity	Home	**34- 0**	**4,626**	**Davies (5)**	**Devereux (2), Eyres, Faimalo, McKenzie, Wright**
17 Workington Town (Regal Trophy 1)	Home	**26- 8**	**4,829**	**Davies (4), Currier**	**Currier, Devereux, D. Hulme, Wright**
23 Carlisle (Regal Trophy 2)	Away	30-16	2,000	Davies (3)	Tait (2), Faimalo, Sarsfield, Wright, Davies
DECEMBER					
1 Featherstone Rovers (Regal Trophy 3)	Home	**34-22**	**6,555**	**Davies (5)**	**Davies (2), Sarsfield, Holliday, Tait, D. Hulme**
4 Bradford Northern	Away	14-36	3,624	Davies	Wynne (3)
8 Wigan	Home	14-23	7,788	**Davies (3)**	**Wynne, D. Hulme**
15 Wakefield Trinity (match abandoned)	Away	8- 0	3,500		Wynne, Sarsfield
21 St Helens (Regal Trophy semi)	Wigan	18-10	6,376	Davies (3)	Wright, Currier, Faimalo
26 Warrington	Home	20- 8	9,975		**Devereux (2), Davies, Eyres, Smith**
JANUARY					
1 St Helens	Home	22-24	13,072	Davies	Devereux (2), Currier, Dowd, Eyres
5 Castleford	Home	**4-14**	**5,279**		Wynne
11 Leeds (Regal Trophy Final)	Wigan	24- 0	15,023	Davies (3) dg, Holliday dg	Davies, Holliday, Tait, Sorensen
19 Hull	Home	**22-20**	**5,552**	**Davies (5)**	**Devereux, Tait, Currier**
FEBRUARY					
2 St Helens (Challenge Cup 1)	Home	**2-10**	**12,776**	**Davies**	
19 Wakefield Trinity		4-12	4,300	Davies (2)	
23 Swinton	Away	38-14	1,980	Davies (7)	Currier (2), Davies, Wright, Devereux, D. Hulme
MARCH					
1 Halifax	Home	**18- 8**	**5,400**	**Davies**	**Devereux (3), D. Hulme**
8 Leeds	Away	28-40	9,799	Devereux (4)	Devereux (3), Tait (2)
15 Hull Kingston Rovers	Away	8-10	3,744	Devereux (2)	P. Hulme
22 Bradford Northern	Home	**10-17**	**4,500**	**Holliday (3)**	**Spruce**
29 Featherstone Rovers	Away	2-28	3,438	Davies (2)	
APRIL					
5 Salford	Home	20-24	3,800	**Devereux, Holliday**	**Devereux (2), Critchley, P. Hulme**
12 Hull	Away	36-20	4,450	Devereux (4)	Devereux (4), Howard, Wright, Holliday
17 Warrington	Away	8-19	6,187	Devereux (2)	Devereux
20 St Helens	Home	**23-28**	**7,227**	**Devereux (5), Holliday dg**	**McKenzie (2), Devereux**
26 Wigan (Premiership 1)	Away	16-42	12,547	Devereux (2)	Eyres, Currier, Carbert

Players total number of games and points 1991/92 season

	Played	Goals	Tries	Points
Paul Atcheson	5			0
Brian Carbert	3		1	4
Jason Critchley	7		1	4
Andy Currier	29	7	9	50
Paul Davidson	2			0
Jonathan Davies	24	(1dg) 73	13	199
John Devereux	27	20	33	172
Barry Dowd	21		2	8
Richie Eyres	29		6	24
Esene Faimalo	24		4	16
Joe Grima	14			0
Neil Holding	3			0
Les Holliday	28	(2dg) 4	3	22
Harvey Howard	17			0
David Hulme	25		8	32
Paul Hulme	27		2	8
Chris Kelly	2			0
Emosi Koloto	19		1	4
David Marsh	3			0
Steve McCurrie	6			0
Phil McKenzie	22		3	12
Paul Moriarty	12			0
Tony Myler	8		2	8
Mark Sarsfield	23		3	12
David Smith	22			0
Se'e Solomona	14		2	8
Kurt Sorensen	22			0
Stuart Spruce	24		3	12
Alan Tait	30		9	36
Darren Wright	35		12	48
Steve Wynne	13		6	24

First Division	Games	Won	Drawn	Lost	For	Against	Points
Wigan	26	22	0	4	645	307	44
St Helens	26	17	2	7	550	338	36
Castleford	26	15	2	9	558	365	32
Warrington	26	15	0	11	507	431	30
Leeds	26	14	1	11	515	408	29
Wakefield Trinity	26	13	1	12	400	435	27
Halifax	26	12	0	14	618	566	24
Widnes	**26**	**12**	**0**	**14**	**511**	**477**	**24**
Hull Kingston Rovers	26	12	0	14	379	466	24
Salford	26	11	0	15	480	587	22
Bradford Northern	26	11	0	15	476	513	22
Hull	26	11	0	15	468	526	22
Featherstone Rovers	26	11	0	15	449	570	22
Swinton	26	3	0	23	254	853	6

7) 1992/93 season "End of an Era"

At the Club's AGM during the summer of 1992, it was announced that a £20,000 profit had been made during the previous season. It was nothing to write home about given the world-record sale of Martin Offiah. Indeed, the financial plight of the Club would cast a shadow over the 1992/93 season. Average attendances at Naughton Park had fallen once again from 7,518 in 1990/91 down to 6,625 in the 1991/92 season. There were surprising changes of both first-team coach and also playing personnel in the summer of 1992. Prop-forward Joe Grima left to join Keighley Cougars (the Third Division club had already adapted an American-style tag name before the birth of Super League). 'Smokin Joe' publicly thanked Widnes fans for the support they had given him in his four years at the Club. Two fringe players Steve Wynn and Jason Critchley were exchanged for former Welsh RU international winger Adrian Hadley with Salford.

Most surprising was an exchange deal done with Leeds for Widnes-born scrum-half Bobby Goulding, with Scottish full-back Alan Tait uniting again with Doug Laughton. Goulding who had been player-of-the-year in the 1991/92 season apparently had an altercation with Doug. It seemed that Phil Larder the Chemics new first-team coach, saw David Hulme more of a stand-off half than a scrum half. Despite the years Hulme had been scrum-half for Widnes, Larder wrote in the programme for the opening league game at home to Castleford on August 30th.

"I have always thought that Widnes have required an organising scrum half. This is no criticism of David Hulme who has been one of the backbones of the Widnes Club. But I feel that David's competitiveness, support play and defensive qualities have been inhibited when he has had to organise.

I will never forget David's contribution to that great Test win in Sydney in 1988 when he played stand-off outside Andy Gregory. Bobby Goulding fits the bill perfectly. Bobby had already proved himself at the highest level being one of the stars of the 1990 Lions Tour and he is still only twenty."

Former Oldham player Larder had been part of the international set-up before joining Widnes. He must have felt vindicated as Hulme and Goulding in an impressive debut, both scored tries in a 16-6 victory. His signing for Widnes had been featured on the front-page of the August 20th edition of the *WWN*. There was a picture of him and his bride alongside Frank Myler. Bobby Goulding had signed for Widnes on his Wedding Day! With Larder's arrival, Frank was either promoted or relegated to the role of "manager". It's not for me to judge events at Naughton Park in 1992, but I cannot help think that the Club did not want to sack a legend for the previous season's abysmal ending. I may be wrong and I hope I am!

The Chemics also won their first away league game at Hull K.R by 16 points to 2. In particularly good early-season form was Richie Eyres, who added two tries to one he scored against Castleford. He did not score any of nine Widnes tries in a 52-8 thrashing of Second Division Carlisle at home in the Lancashire Cup on September 13th. Adrian Hadley scored his first try for the Club, whilst Paul Hulme and Stuart Spruce who played at right-centre, both scored a brace. Spruce caught Paul Cook's eye as did the returning Tony Myler. It was to be virtually the

Maestro's last hurrah. He was only to play a handful games in the 1992/93 season which was to be his final one. What a player, and he still had all his skills intact to he end of his career. Part of Paul Cook's match-report read:

"Tony Myler back from yet another serious injury, illuminated proceedings with his mesmeric ball skills while Stuart Spruce handled the centre role with flair and confidence."

Frank Myler still retained his column in the *WWN*. In echoes of what he had stated early in the previous season, Frank enthused the week after the Carlisle game "Best is yet to come!". What came immediately were three tough games and three defeats. Against Bradford at home on September 20th, The Chemics were leading 6-2 at half-time through yet another Richie Eyres try and Jonathan Davies goal. They looked in command and could have been further ahead. In the second-half when pressing for another try, Bradford winger Gerald Cordle intercepted a pass and raced 95 yards to score at the other end. The complexion of the match changed as Bradford went on to win 24-12.

The next loss was at Wigan in another early season encounter televised by Sky. The previous season both sides scored four tries in a tough, but relatively free-scoring game. The 1992/93 game was even tougher with ferocious and ruthless tackling from both sides. Wigan held an 8-2 lead going into the closing stages thanks to Frano Botica, He had not only kicked two goals, but had scored the only try of the game late in the first-half. As in the Premiership game at the end of the previous season, it was Martin Offiah who put the game beyond the reach of his former team-mates. In this own 25 and with the clock ticking down, Jonathan Davies ambitiously chipped the ball ahead. It was picked up by Martin who raced through the Widnes defence to score a converted try and make the final score 14-2. Five nights later the Chemics lost narrowly again 8-10 in another hard-fought low-scoring game at St Helens in the second round of the Lancashire Cup.

black & white

Twelve months is a long time in rugby league. This time last year we featured an interview in 'Black & White' with Bobby Goulding, the occasion being the visit to Naughton Park of his new club, Leeds. We also recalled his appearance for Widnes in a charity match in 1987 and described it as possibly 'the only time we will ever see Bobby Goulding in a Widnes jersey.'

At the start of another season we now have the pleasure of recording Bobby's signing for Widnes and wishing him good luck in this new

Local lad . . . Bobby Goulding.

Bobby Goulding proved to a great signing by Phil Larder before the start of the 1992/93 season.

Winning ways were resumed spectacularly on October 4th in the return fixture against Hull Kingston Rovers at Naughton Park. As in the Lancashire Cup first round against Carlisle, the Chemics racked up 52 points and this time didn't concede any. Star of the show was John Devereux who showed the form that had brought him 33 tries in just 27 games the previous season. He scored his first four of the 1992/93 season. Great Britain were to play Australia in the 1992 World Cup Final on October 24th at Wembley. Paul Cook in his match-report expressed his opinion that Devereux should be included in the GB side. "Devs" had a patchy start to the 1992/93 season, not scoring in the three previous games he had played. He and Bobby Goulding had also incurred somewhat unjustly a two-match suspension for an incident in the opening league game against Castleford.

Adrian Hadley scored his second try for Widnes against Hull K.R. Even so one Widnes supporter did not see him as the player to replace Martin Offiah. A letter published in the same October 8th edition of the *WWN* of the report on the game against Hull Kingston was headed **"Prayer's to sign a wingman"**. The supporter urged the re-signing of David Myers who had lost his place at Wigan since they had signed Offiah. It seemed that Phil Larder had already signed Myers by the time the letter was published. Myers made a try-scoring debut the following week at Castleford, but played not on the left but the right-wing.

In the programme for the next home game against Halifax on October 18th, Phil Larder congratulated John Devereux and Richie Eyres for their inclusion in the Great Britain squad for the forthcoming World Cup Final against Australia. Eyres in particular had been in great form. He had also bulked up because of training methods that Larder had introduced since taking over. Bobby Goulding perhaps should also have been in the squad. He was proving to be a great signing. Not only had he been the organiser that Phil Larder hoped he would be, in the absence of Jonathan Davies he kicked four goals as the Chemics ground out a 20-8 win over Halifax. His work-rate in the game was also reminiscent of the Hulme brothers.

The form of Goulding and Eyres may have been consistent early in the season, but the team as a whole was not. In the programme for the Halifax game Phil Larder also intimated that he and his coaching staff were working hard to bring more consistency. More consistency did come, but later rather than sooner. The week after the victory over Halifax his team slumped to their fourth league defeat of the season. It was a hefty one, as they were comprehensively thrashed away by Doug Laughton's Leeds team 48-16. It was indeed a horror show as Paul Cook described, and he did not use the sending-off of forwards Harvey Howard and Steve McCurrie as an excuse. Even so, he was more scathing of what was said of the Widnes team in the match-programme than the performance. He wrote:

"Having been beaten so heavily, it might sound like sour grapes to have a gripe about Leeds and their supporters but I'm going to have a go anyway. Having to listen to fans bemoaning how Widnes have slipped and also reading in the programme that there remains a nagging feeling Widnes should have won more trophies is a bit much coming from a team with a trophy cabinet like a Moscow supermarket - full of empty shelves.

It must be great having a fortune to spend every summer on transfers and contracts and then lecture the most consistent team of the last 20 years on why they should have won more trophies."

Letters from supporters were published in the *WWN* in October 1992 giving various opinions on the team's inconsistent form. One supporter wrote that Emosi Koloto and Phil McKenzie should be restored to the first-team. Another stated that Larder had the team playing like "battering rams" and not utilising their speed and skill. and he was selecting players out position. One supporter wrote that Jonathan Davies was "not a full-back". The Welsh superstar had actually played at left-centre in the home victory over Halifax and in the defeat at Leeds. In the Sport section of the November 5th edition of the *WWN* following the defeat at Leeds, an article headlined "**MYLER INJURY SHOCK**" began: "Tony Myler's brilliant career is back in balance". Tony had been injured again at Leeds and it was to be his last game for Widnes. It was apt that he had scored a try in his last appearance at Naughton Park in the game against Halifax.

Making his debut for the Chemics at stand-off in their next home game was short-term Australian signing Julian O'Neill. He scored two tries as Third Division Ryedale-York were beaten 46-4 in the first round of the Regal Trophy. Forwards Les Holliday and Paul Moriarty also scored two tries each. Phil Larder re-shuffled his team again for the visit of Wigan on Friday November 13th. Julian O'Neill was shifted to right-centre and Darren Wright and Andy Currier formed a partnership on the left-flank. The two stalwarts had requested transfers having been dropped by Phil Larder earlier in the season. Again, the game was televised by Sky and again the Chemics took Wigan all the way. Future Widnes Vikings coach Dennis Betts scored a converted try at the death to make the final score 18-6 in Wigan's favour.

Phil Larder wrote in the 1992/93 season home game programmes. but not in the *WWN*.

Missing from the line-up against Wigan and out of action until the New Year was Jonathan Davies. He had had incurred a groin injury in the Regal Trophy game against York. Perhaps the next league game at Sheffield may have been won had Davies played. In a high-scoring game, the Chemics scored six tries against the Eagles five on a rain-soaked pitch. It was though the goal-kicking of Eagles half-back Mark Aston that edged them to victory and put Widnes into the bottom half of Division One. The Chemics goal-kicking duties were shared by Currier and Goulding in the absence of Davies. The two goal-kickers combined to create the most spectacular try of the game. After 25 minutes Goulding passed to Currier five yards from the Widnes line. Andy again playing on the left-wing, scorched 90 yards to score. He scored another two and nearly snatched a 32-32 draw for his team with a conversion attempt in the last minute.

On December 1st at Naughton Park in a Tuesday evening league game, the Chemics had to come back twice to defeat Wakefield Trinity 16-10. It was to be the only league game of the month owing to postponements and having to play two Regal Trophy ties. After his hat-trick at Sheffield, Andy Currier was back in his more accustomed right-centre position. John Devereux carried on from where Andy had left off at Sheffield by scoring two playing on the left-wing. His first came when Emosi Koloto came on as substitute in his first home appearance of the season and gave the Welshman a perfectly timed pass. His second came when he typically powered his way through the Trinity defence.

Tries were coming on the left-wing again! There had been a paucity of them since Martin Offiah's departure. Mark Sarsfield only scored three in 23 games in the 1991/92 season, and Adrian Hadley had only scored two in 10 games in the 1992/93 season. The figures were not necessarily an indictment on the two players. Hadley had proved himself at Salford and as a Welsh Rugby Union international to be a fine wingman. During the 1992/93 season Sarsfield scored an impressive total of 16 tries in 23 games for the Widnes A-team. Ironically, in the first-half of the 1992/93 season, Martin Offiah was experiencing the leanest try-scoring spell of his career. He had scored only six tries in the 12 games he played for Wigan by the start of December He never even scored on his return to Naughton Park as he seemed destined to do.

The following Sunday Second Division Rochdale Hornets were comfortably dispatched by 30 points to 2 at Naughton Park, as the Chemics progressed to the third round of the Regal Trophy.David Hulme unusually played at full-back, after Stuart Spruce was declared unfit on the morning of the game. Like Andy Currier and Darren Wright earlier in the season, he had put in a transfer request. Paul Hulme was amongst the try-scorers against Rochdale as was Welsh forward Paul Moriarty. Moriarty for the first time since Doug Laughton signed him, was enjoying a good injury-free run. Up to this point in the season, he was the only player who had not missed a game. He was showing good form and fitting well into Phil Larder's team.

Larder perhaps still had not found his ideal line-up. The decision to play David Hulme at full-back was perhaps his most extreme decision in switching players from position to position. Even King Kurt had found himself on the substitutes bench a couple of times. On December 29th Widnes relinquished their hold on the Regal Trophy so brilliantly won the previous season. They lost 10-21 in the third round at Bradford. Not only were they out of the Regal Trophy, but they had only won five and lost six of their league games as 1993 dawned. In his match-report Paul Cook commented on the patchy and inconsistent form that had dogged Widnes since the start of the season. He sang a different tune when reporting on the first game of 1993 away at Salford on January 6th. He wrote:

"This was like the Championship years re-visited. Widnes were in prime form - the ball frequently going through half a dozen pair of hands and Salford on the end of a good hiding. It was far and away Widnes' best display of the season, even taking into account those mighty battles with Wigan and St Helens earlier in the campaign.

Emosi Koloto was again superb as was Bobby Goulding who took the ball up to the Salford defensive line far than he has been doing. Widnes reaped the benefits when the defenders were committed. At least half a dozen other players had outstanding games with Currier, Devereux, Eyres and Faimalo all playing out of their skin."

Four days after the 48-12 annihilation of Salford the Chemics travelled to Hull. They could not have given a better example of their inconsistency. They looked completely bereft of ideas and inspiration as they slumped to a 4-20 defeat. They had not won two successive league games since the very start of season. Also, before Christmas it had been publicised that the Club might have to sell Jonathan Davies because they were cash-strapped. There were rumours of dressing room unrest and Les Holliday was another player in January 1993 to put in a transfer request. The Chemics had to play a Preliminary round in the 1993 Challenge Cup at home in mid-week after the defeat at Hull.

A decisive victory over Second Division Swinton was perhaps expected, but even a 62-14 massacre may not have indicated that the second-half of the season would be much better than the first. A 56-10 home thrashing of Sheffield Eagles at the weekend when league fixtures resumed was a different matter. The start of Paul Cook's match-report was prophetic. He wrote:

"It's difficult to evaluate just how significant this win might prove to be. How Widnes follow it up will provide a real guide, but on the face of it this was an astonishing performance."

When Widnes hammered Swinton in the Challenge Cup in January 1993, it started a a great run of form. However, Jim Mills was compelled to write about the Club's financial plight in the match-programme.

It was indeed an astonishing performance. And it proved as Paul Cook implied to be significant. At last, a second successive league victory by 10 points to 8 was achieved at Warrington in another mid-week game re-arranged because the Boxing Day fixture was cancelled. Widnes followed up their two straight league victories to win their next six and also surged through to the 1993 Challenge Cup Final. From defeating Swinton in the competition on Wednesday 13th January, they went 14 more games unbeaten. Phil Larder's Widnes team really started to gel.

When part of the Great Britain set-up, Larder had studied training sessions by the Australians, and had introduced coaching methods at Widnes that were coming to fruition. As already written, Richie Eyres had bulked up and was playing better than ever. Larder also seemed to be more decided about his best starting line-up. It was no doubt a fillip in January 1993 when the Club announced they would be not be selling Jonathan Davies. In the games against Swinton and Sheffield, he had scored five tries collectively playing on the left-wing. Jonathan played at stand-off half when Widnes faced Second Division Whitehaven away in the first round of the Challenge Cup on January 31st. Four years after joining Widnes he was to have his most prolonged run in the position. David Myers was back on the left-wing and scored a try. Andy Currier did even better and scored two. After dropping Currier earlier in the season, Phil Larder was now describing him as "the best centre in the game". Larder's team cruised into the second round winning by 20 points to 8.

On February 7th Hull were the visitors to Naughton Park and the defeat in the away fixture a month earlier was avenged. The scoreline was virtually reversed as the Chemics won 22-4. After scoring a try in his come-back game at Whitehaven Dave Myers played on the right-wing in the absence of John Devereux. On the left wing was Mark Sarsfield who scored a first-half try after a fine beak by David Hulme. It was the 16th try of the season scored on the left-wing. The try of the match though was scored by Andy Currier whose form had earned him a place in the Great Britain squad to play France later in the month. Paul Cook's description of Currier's try against Hull I think illustrates what a great player Andy was at his best. He wrote:

"Andy Currier got the ball rolling with one of the tries of the season. He received a pass some 50 yards out and really pinned his ears back for the line. One dummy and a good hand-off later, he was flying down the touchline for a score. The try really encapsulated Currier's form at present.

He didn't slow down looking for support in case he was caught, he didn't believe he would be caught. The try brought the crowd to life and confirmed - if further confirmation was needed - Currier is the best centre in the league."

In the *WWN* on the Thursday following the victory over Hull, Phil Larder stated with some justification that his team "'were finally getting it right". At the weekend the Chemics were to face Sheffield Eagles away in the second round of the Challenge Cup. Phil Larder also stated with some justification in the programme for the Hull game that the tie at Sheffield "will be be no-walk-over". He implied that the hammering his team had given to Sheffield at home in January would have no bearing on the outcome. Most Widnes supporters may have shared Larder's reservations. After all, Sheffield had narrowly beaten the Chemics on their home turf in November. They had also beaten Doug Laughton's teams a couple of times in recent seasons. A tough, close battle could have been reasonably expected.

Eleven tries were scored as in the league fixture before Christmas, and it was Widnes who scored 10 of them. Phil Larder's team did not walk, they trampled over a hapless Sheffield outfit. They repeated the 46-point winning margin of the league game, with both teams scoring just four points less than they had done at Naughton Park. The Widnes tries were equally divided by Stuart Spruce, John Devereux, Andy Currier, Darren Wright and Jonathan Davies. All five players scored two tries each and Davies and Bobby Goulding kicked three goals each. Not a point was scored by the forwards, but in his match-report Paul Cook wrote:

"But while the threequarters grabbed the glory, the forwards again provided the platform. Koloto had another of those inspired days when he looked best second-rower around. Faimalo and Sorensen worked hard and Eyres took several chances to hit the gaps. Paul Hulme was also having a big game until his match was unfortunately cut short."

As Widnes had to play Warrington away on January 20th because of the postponement of the Boxing Day fixture, they were to play St Helens on the evening of Wednesday February 17th in yet another re-arranged game. With Wembley in their sights having reached the Challenge Cup third round the previous Sunday, it would have been no surprise if the Chemics had succumbed to a side still in the Championship race. Far from succumbing, they demonstrated to St Helens that they also would have been in the Championship race had they have gelled earlier in the season. For the seventh game in succession Andy Currier scored a try, whist his co-centre Darren Wright scored again in a 26-8 victory. The two tall, classy and pacey centres were back working in harness as they had done so often in the previous six years.

Inspired Widnes cut above Eagles

JUST how high should we raise our hopes?

There was every reason to believe on Sunday that this, at last, could be the year.

After several seasons when the Chemics were favourites to reach Wembley but were always denied, they moved smoothly into the Silk Cut Challenge Cup quarter-finals

Sheffield Eagles 6 Widnes 52
BY PAUL COOK

Sunday only because they turned up. In reality, they were a beaten team in next to no time.

No-one from Widnes had a bad game and several players were, once again, outstanding.

In recent weeks it has become second nature to praise the

from the tunnel just to raise the temperature a little more.

Sheffield, I imagine, would rather he hadn't as they were submerged beneath waves of attacks from the opening minutes.

Ten tries tell their own story, with all the scorers doubling up.

Currier, Devereux, Davies, Stuart Spruce and Darren Wright all notched up two tries

At Wakefield at the weekend, Phil Larder's remorseless Widnes machine scored five tries in the first-half before going on to win 36-18. In contrast to the cup-tie at Sheffield, four of the six Widnes tries were scored by forwards. Paul Moriarty scored two of them, whilst hooker Steve McCurrie and substitute forward Harvey Howard shared the other two. If the early-season problems on the field had been ironed out, the off-field financial problems had most certainly not. Indeed, a 'Widnes In Need' campaign was launched. An article in the February 18th edition of the *WWN* headlined **"CHEMICS IN CRISIS"** began:

"Widnes have launched an urgent fund-raising campaign to find £250,000 for the end of this season. An extraordinary meeting of the club heard money was needed to cover players contracts and creditors. The bleak financial situation was outlined to 600 members at the Queens Hall on Monday."

In the following week's edition in an article by reporter David Bettley, Phil Larder commented on the weekend's third round Challenge Cup-tie away to Hull Kingston Rovers. Though Rovers were bottom of Division One, he urged caution and expressed concern that some Widnes supporters believed a semi-final place was a formality. The heavy pitch, the driving rain and a strong ice-cold wind conspired to produce the most atrocious conditions imaginable. It was so bad that Larder asked the referee at half-time to cancel the game. Some Widnes players were apparently suffering from exposure. Hull Kingston were having the same problems, and their Australian full-back David Liddiard was considered to be too cold to resume in the second-half. The conditions also proved to be a leveller and vindicated Phil Larder's pre-match call for caution. Playing with the Arctic wind in the first-half, the Chemics were ahead at the interval through a try by full-back Stuart Spruce. In the last 10 minutes Hull K.R winger Paul Fletcher scored an equalising try. The conversion attempt went perilously close to being successful.

The replay at Naughton Park three nights later on March 3rd, was by no means a formality either. Indeed, the Humberside team were good value for their 5-2 interval lead. In the second-half, the Chemics took command. John Devereux led the revival with a great 60-yard break and then Kurt Sorensen gave a short pass to Harvey Howard who powered over. Richie Eyres in effect sealed the tie when he tore a big hole in the Rovers defence to score a second Widnes try. Richie was still committed to the Chemics cause, although he had become yet another Widnes player to ask for a transfer a few weeks earlier! Rovers scored a late, converted try but Phil Larder's team were through to the semi-final winning 16-11.

The Chemics were to play Leeds on March 13th at Central Park in the semi-final. Though Widnes were on a great run of form, so were Doug Laughton's team. Their season had followed a similar pattern to that of Widnes. Before Christmas they had also lost seven league games, but had also lost only once since. Leeds were therefore favourites as they had been in the previous season's Regal Trophy Final at Central Park. What may also have made Leeds favourites was the hiding they had given Widnes in November. The Chemics had two untimely injuries in the games against Hull Kingston Rovers. Forwards Esene Faimalo and Paul Moriarty were both out with knee injuries. It was wretched luck for the stockily-built New Zealander and for the tall Welshman. They had been playing consistently and had established themselves in Phil Larder's team. Faimalo had only missed four games rior to his injury in the drawn game at Hull K.R. whilst Moriarity's luck with njuries it seemed had changed completely. He had missed just one game since the tart of the season.

It was perhaps still fresh on Doug Laughton's mind how Widnes had lestroyed his Leeds team in the 1992 Regal Trophy Final. It could not happen again ould it? Lightning did strike twice and it struck almost twice as hard as it did in 992. As in the previous season's Regal Trophy showdown, it was again in the econd-half that Widnes opened the floodgates. In the 1993 Challenge Cup semi-inal, the second-half deluge was even more severe. This time around the Chemics cored six tries of which four were converted to total 32 unanswered second-half oints. As in the slaying of Sheffield in the second round, the backs scored all seven ries but the forwards laid the foundations as Widnes booked their place at Vembley in great style. David Myers scored the only first-half try capitalising on a in-point Bobby Goulding cross-kick.

Goulding won the man-of-the-match award, and it was also a "bomb" by lobby which resulted in the first of the tries scored after the interval by John Devereux. Darren Wright though not amongst the scorers as at Sheffield, made a hrilling 40-yard run before passing to Jonathan Davies who scored the first of two econd-half tries. Jonathan also kicked two tremendous touch-line conversions. Andy Currier's try was a great individual effort, throwing a dummy then slicing hrough the Leeds cover. Full-back Stuart Spuce added to his try in the third round, nd David Myers added to his first-half try near the end to complete a 39-4 hrashing. In the forwards Kurt Sorensen and Harvey Howard dominated up front. .eeds also had nobody commited to their cause as the Hulme brothers were ommited to the Widnes cause. The *WWN's* breath-taking display" phrase aptly lescribed the Chemics performance.

A jubilant Widnes dressing room after the 1993 Challenge Cup semi-final victory over Leeds.

Doug Laughton's shell-shocked Leeds team were at Naughton Park th
following Wednesday evening for the return league fixture. Phil Larder's team
rubbed salt in the Leeds wound winning 19-8. It was not a repeat of the Challeng
Cup thrashing, but it was comfortable enough. Perhaps some Widnes supporter
had some sympathy for the man who done so much for the Club. Certainly, Ph
Larder did, he wrote in the match-programme for the league fixture:

"Sunday morning, I could not help feeling sorry for Dougie Laughton and hi
Leeds players to get so close to Wembley only to lose in a semi-final must surely be th
worst feeling in rugby league."

There was nothing comfortable about the Chemics victory away at Leig
the following weekend. Captain Paul Hulme more noted for topping the tackle
count weekly, led by example and scored a late try to snatch a narrow 14-11 win fo
his team. At Naughton Park on March 26th Widnes defeated Salford 38-22 in mor
customary style. John Devereux who had scored a try in both games against Leed
and at Leigh, scored two this time from the right-centre position. It was 38-4 half
way through the second-half when as Paul Cook inferred in his match-report, th
minds of the players may have had other considerations and therefore eased of
The "considerations" to which Cook was alluding were of course a showdow
against Wigan in the Challenge Cup Final and avoiding injury for the game. I
addition to the injuries of Moriarty and Faimalo, Emosi Koloto had not playe
since the Challenge Cup semi-final.

It was perhaps understandable being out of the Championship race as we
as Wembley-bound, that form would dip in the last five league games. On the las
day of March, the 15-match unbeaten run stretching back to January ended with
0-28 thrashing at Bradford. That heavy defeat was compounded with another 6-4
hammering the following week at Halifax. The two defeats may not have bee
surprising, though perhaps the margins were. If victories in those games were no
essential, it was essential that £500,000 was raised to allay the Club's financia
problems. On the front-page of the April 1st edition of the *WWN*, the leadin
article was about the financial plight of Widnes RLFC. it was headlined **"ONE W
HAVE TO WIN"** and the article began:

"As pre-Wembley fever hits Widnes, with fans queueing for RL Cup Final ticket
from 6.30am on Saturday, officials have made it clear that £500,000 is needed to sav
the rugby club. So far £90,000 has been raised chiefly from company donations and from
the sale from Win-a-Line £5 weekly draw tickets. The half-million-pound target is seen a
the minimum Widnes needs to stay in business."

On Good Friday April 9th Phil Larder's team put the defeats in the tw
previous league games and the Club's financial situation behind them. They looke
more committed as they defeated Warrington 26-14. The star player for th
Chemics was Steve McCurrie, who scored three of the five Widnes tries. McCurri
still not yet 20-years of age, had always played with authority and maturity beyon
his years. He was selected the previous month for the Great Britain side tha
defeated France. Though he did not play hooker against Warrington, he was th
main factor as to why Phil McKenzie was no longer in the first-team. It was n
surprise that the Chemics lost to Championship-chasing St Helens on Easte

Monday. They did though play better in the 18-29 defeat than they had done in the heavy losses at Bradford and Halifax.

It was a surprise that the final league at home to Leigh on April 28th was lost. It was surprising in the sense that the Chemics held a 16-4 half-time lead. It was another case of the minds of the players being focused on Wembley. The defeat was academic as Widnes finished fourth in the Division One table. One positive of the Leigh game was that Esene Faimalo was fit again, The New Zealander scored one of the Widnes tries and would be vital in the Challenge Cup Final. Widnes were to play Doug Laughton's Leeds team the following week in the first round of the Premiership at Naughton Park. Paul Moriarty was back in the side, but sustained another injury which ruled him out of playing at Wembley. Widnes gave a good first-half performance and led 10-8 at the break. With greater incentive for victory perhaps, Leeds pulled away in the second-half to win 22-10. They also dealt out some rough stuff in Paul Cook's opinion. He wrote that referee John Connolly was too lenient as did some home supporters who heaped vitriol on him at the end of the game.

The stage was set for the Challenge Cup Final against Wigan at Wembley stadium on May 1st. Wigan had again won the Championship and were going for their fourth successive double and their sixth successive Challenge Cup. They were the favourites, but one man who had belief in a Widnes victory was Vin Karalius. An interview with the man who had kick-started the reign of 'The Cup Kings' back in the early 1970s, was published in the April 29th edition of the *WWN*. Vin was full of praise for many of the Widnes players. He spoke highly of Kurt Sorensen whom he brought to the Club in his brief second reign as team-coach in 1984. Vin said of Kurt "he's been one of the greatest forwards in the game". He also described the Hulme brothers as "a credit to the game and to the Club". Vin further gave the opinion that Andy Currier and Darren Wright "have come of age and both top players - two of the best centres in the game. He gave further praise to John Devereux and Stuart Spruce.

In order to bolster his squad, Phil Larder wanted Australian Julian O'Neill back from Australia. It was a move reminiscent of what Vin Karalius did back in 1975. Australian winger Chris Anderson like O'Neill, was a short-term signing who left the Club with a few months of the season remaining. Vin had Anderson flown back for the 1975 final against Warrington. Getting O'Neill back was more difficult and it took the intervention of Halton MP Gordon Oakes to ensure O'Neill was granted a permit in 20 days rather than 20 weeks! As it transpired, all reported injuries cleared up for the Challenge Cup Final with the exception of Moriarty and Koloto. A near full-strength Widnes team was ready to confront Wigan at Wembley. Julian O'Neill was therefore only one of the substitutes. The Widnes line-up was:

Stuart Spruce, John Devereux, Andy Currier, Darren Wright, David Myers, Jonathan Davies, Bobby Goulding, Kurt Sorensen, Paul Hulme, Harvey Howard, Richie Eyres, Esene Faimalo, David Hulme. Substitutes **Julian O'Neill** and **Steve McCurrie.**

After seven minutes play Bobby Goulding helped the Chemics get off to a dream start. Widnes had got to within the Wigan 25 when he changed the point of the attack making a short run to the blind side. He fed the supporting Richie Eyres who forced his way over the line. Jonathan Davies kicked a magnificent conversion to give Widnes the initiative. It was surrendered four minutes later when lost possession allowed Wigan into an attacking position. Prop-forward Kelvin Skerret forced his way out of attempts by Darren Wright and Stuart Spruce to stop him to go over for a converted try. Widnes re-gained the lead within another six minutes of play. Esene Faimalo and Harvey Howard took their team to within 30 yards of the Wigan line. After Howard was tackled, Kurt Sorensen was the first receiver from the ensuing play-the-ball. The King did better than merely drive nearer to the Wigan posts. This was after all, his Grand Finale. I'll leave it to Paul Cook to describe what happened next.

"The man who struck was Kurt Sorensen and if there's anybody in the game who wasn't delighted then they must have a heart of stone. Sorensen took a short pass up to the Wigan defensive line and like a tank with a mind of its own rumbled through the tackles of Botica and Hampson before touching down. Sorensen's legendary status at Widnes is already established, but if this was truly his last game for the Club, then he couldn't have gone out on a bigger note or bigger stage."

Had it gone according to the script Kurt's try would have been the winning one, and perhaps Widnes skipper Paul Hulme would have allowed him to collect the trophy. Sadly, a disastrous error by John Devereux allowed Wigan to draw level again. Wigan half-back Shaun Edwards sent a long kick into Widnes territory and towards Devereux's wing. Just 10 yards from the Widnes try-line Devereux spilled the ball when he was tackled by Martin Offiah. The former Widnes wingman threw an inside pass to supporting team-mate Dean Bell who scored. It was tough on Devereux, as he had another great season and was for the second successive year the team's leading try-scorer. Frano Botica needless to say converted, and before half-time kicked a penalty to give his side a 14-12 lead at the interval.

Wigan opened the second-half on the front foot, and scored a try within two minutes of the game resuming. A break by second-row forward Dennis Betts took his team deep into Widnes territory. With the Chemics defence scattered, Dean Bell this time off-loaded for substitute Sam Panapa to go under the posts for a converted try. It could have been a bad psychological blow for Phil Larder's team. But the gritty Chemics stuck at it, and got back within firing range with a Jonathan Davies penalty. With the heat soaring up into the 80s it might have been expected for gaps to appear in both defences. As it unfolded, the game became an even a greater war of attrition than it been from the kick-off. The fact that three of the game's five tries were scored by forwards using to their strength to score and one was the result of a mistake said everything.

There were no further tries, and Widnes could not get the field position to mount any sustained pressure on the Wigan line. The score stayed at 20-14 in Wigan's favour as they retained the Challenge Cup for the sixth successive season. As well as temperatures hotting up in the second-half, tempers did also. Richie Eyres showed no gratitude to Martin Offiah for the tries he scored for Widnes when they were team-mates. Because he nearly took Martin's head off, he found himself heading off, becoming the second player to be sent off in a Challenge Cup Final. His dismissal was to say the least, less controversial than his sending-off against St Helens in the 1989 semi-final. Bobby Goulding may well have followed after a high tackle on right-winger Jason Robinson. Despite their indiscretions, the two players had given everything during the game and indeed during the 1992/93 season. Eyres already an accomplished forward with international credentials before Phil Larder came to the Club, was playing better than ever. Goulding was voted by the Widnes supporters club as 'player-of-the-year.'

Not only Eyres and Goulding, but all the Widnes players had given everything in the 1993 Challenge Cup Final. It's just a pity that King Kurt could not have finished his playing days at Widnes with a winner's medal. Even so, his great try is an indelible memory and encapsulated what an indomitable player he was. Widnes seemed to have served notice to Wigan as they had done back in 1987, that they were not going to have things their own way in the coming seasons. Life after Doug Laughton and Martin Offiah seemed have begun in earnest under Phil Larder's leadership.

Captain Paul Hulme in action during the 1993 Challenge Cup Final. Esene Faimalo to his left.

Indeed, Larder had spoken during the team's great 15-game unbeaten run about having "a tilt at the Championship" in the 1993/94 season. Paul Cook concluded his report by expressing the hope that Widnes would not have to wait another nine years to "put the record straight". It seemed to be by no means a far fetched hope. An article in the following week's *WWN* was not unreasonably headlined **"We'll be back"**. There were quotes from several of the players who had taken Wigan all the way. One of them was by the retiring Kurt Sorensen. Kurt was quoted as saying:

"This is a platform for us to build on. We're on our way back. We've made a good account of ourselves this season amid adversity. We're on our way back."

Sadly, Kurt's optimism was misplaced as were the hopes of Paul Cook and Phil Larder. During the summer of 1993, despite the windfall of money from the Challenge Cup Final, the Club's financial problems imploded. Jonathan Davies moved to Warrington without a transfer fee as the Club could not afford his contract. Andy Currier and Richie Eyres were sold to Featherstone and Leeds respectively. Kurt of course was virtually irreplaceable, but his heir apparent Harvey Howard also moved to Leeds early in the 1993/94 season. Although he had not played during the 1992/93 season, Phil McKenzie, another link to the Doug Laughton era, moved on to Workington during the close season. It was perhaps ironic that the dashing hooker never played a game for Widnes under the 10-yard rule which was introduced during the 1992/93 season. Tony Myler only played six games in the 1992/93 season before injury struck yet again. It was a pity that Tony could not have bowed out with Kurt at Wembley in 1993. Barry Dowd, so often Tony's understudy, made just one appearance in the 1992/93 season. Dowd, another player from the Laughton era, also never played for Widnes again. The so often influential Les Holliday was also transferred to Halifax.

When Doug left Widnes after the 1991 Premiership Final and Martin Offiah stated his desire to leave, Paul Cook had asked the question "End of An Era?" It was not quite, but in 1993 it was. Widnes Rugby League Football Club has never been a force in British Rugby League since.

At the start of the 1993/94 season, only the Hulme brothers and Darren Wright of the 1987/88 Championship winning team remained at the Club. It was perhaps symbolic that there was a radical jersey change from the white jersey and black shorts that the team had worn throughout the era of the 'Cup Kings' up until the end of the 1992/93 season. There were still plenty of talented players at the Club in the 1993/94 season, but the retirement of Sorensen and the departures of Davies, Currier and Eyres in particular, perhaps caused too much collateral damage. The Chemics only finished 10th in the First Division and never qualified for the Premiership Trophy play-offs or reached the semi-finals of either the Regal Trophy or the Challenge Cup. Phil Larder resigned as first-team coach and Bobby Goulding and Esene Faimalo were transferred to St Helens and Leeds respectively after the end of the season.

Tony Myler was appointed first-team coach for the 1994/95 season. He was inheriting a difficult situation and he only lasted a year. It was sad that Widnes finished third from the bottom of Division One whilst he was in charge. Widnes needed to finish in the top 10 to avoid relegation. In preparation for the advent of

Super League there was a restructuring of the divisions. In the 1995/96 season Doug Laughton briefly returned. Doug had not been able to deliver any trophies at Leeds. He did get to two Challenge Cup and a Premiership Final, but his teams were beaten convincingly by the mighty Wigan on each occasion. In the final pre-Super League season, Doug showed he'd not lost all his coaching magic. A Widnes team far less talented than his 1989 and 1991 teams, again faced St Helens in the Challenge Cup semi-final in 1996. They put on a brave performance before losing 14-24. It was the last time Widnes played as 'The Chemics' in a Challenge Cup game. Later in 1996, 'Widnes Vikings' were born with the start of the Super League era.

I will always believe that the Chemics as they were known. could have dominated British RL or at least matched Wigan stride for stride until the advent of Super League. I believe the departures of Doug and Martin was the main reason why they did not. And would they have left had the team reached a Challenge Cup Final between 1987 and 1991? And did the World Club Championship triumph in 1989 distract the team not only from a Challenge Cup Final appearance, but a third successive Championship? And despite the departures of Doug and Martin, could Phil Larder have taken the team further but for the financial problems that led to the offloading of his best players? It's all ifs and buts.

Fans overwhelmingly against Davies's departure-

CLUB SLAMMED

You give your views on the controversy

I HAVE been a Widnes supporter for 33 years since leaving school.

tainly Warrington's gain. Thank you for the pleasure you have given us.

EX-WIDNES SUPPORTER OF 33 YEARS
(Name and address

I think one can say regarding the financial problems that basically finished Widnes as a force in British RL, if ever there was a case for 'boom and bust' it was Widnes Rugby League Club between 1987 and 1993. As I finish this book Widnes Vikings are once again outside of Super League. They have also had financial problems simlar to those in the early 1990s. Maybe in the fullness of time they will be a force in British Rugby League. If ever they are, I just cannot conceive that there will anything again like the era I've tried to re-capture in this book. There will never be another Doug Laughton, there will never be another Martin Offiah, there will never be another Kurt Sorensen, nor another Tony Myler, Andy Currier, Darren Wright, Richie Eyres, David and Paul Hulme etc.etc. During the writing of this book Martin Offiah and Kurt Sorensen have been inducted into the Club's 'Hall of Fame'. There will always be debate and dispute as to who should and should not be in the HOF.

I therefore conclude my naming all the players who played for Widnes in those unforgettable seasons between 1987/88 and 1992/93. I also include the first-team coaches in the period. I hope this book commemorates them and is a 'Hall of Fame' in its own right.

Paul Atcheson, Chris Ashurst, Brian Carbert, Jason Critchley, Andy Currier, Paul Davidson, Jonathan Davies, John Devereux, Barry Dowd, Andy Eyres, Richie Eyres, Esene Faimalo, Ian Gormley, Joe Grima, Bobby Goulding, Adrian Hadley, Karle Hammond, Neil Holding, Les Holliday, Harvey Howard, David Hulme, Paul Hulme, Andy Ireland, Brima Kebbie, Chris Kelly, Emosi Koloto, Phil Larder, 'Sir' Douglas Laughton, Ben Lia, Ralph Linton, Chris Lloyd, Steve McCurrie, Phil McKenzie, David Marsh, Paul Moriarty, Dave Myers, Frank Myler, John Myler, Tony Myler, Keith Newton, Martin Offiah, Julian O'Neill, Mike O'Neill, Steve O'Neill, Steve Pickett, Harry Pinner, Duncan Platt, Derek Pyke, Dave Ruane, Mark Sarsfield, Dale Shearer, David Smith, Se'e Solomona, 'King' Kurt Sorensen, Stuart Spruce, Trevor Stockley, Andy Sullivan, Alan Tait, Rick Thackray, Boblin Tuavo, Christian Tyrer, Darren Wright, Steve Wynne.

End of an era?

PAUL COOK

on the day

Widnes

went down

IT might be too soon to be talking about Sunday's defeat in terms of the end of an era, but it was somewhat appropriate that Widnes should go down amid the rumours surrounding this Premiership final.

Five seasons ago it was a Premiership first round tie against Wigan that gave the first inkling that Widnes might be on the

long, but there will be much, much worse that never gets punished. Hull kicked deep into Widnes territory and from the resulting possession they manoeuvred the position from which substitute Gary Nolan scored the decisive try.

Eastwood's goal was merely icing on the celebration cake as Hull were home and dry. When the final whistle sounded, Martin Offiah failed to acknowledge the fans who had provided great support even with all the rumours being bandied about. He also didn't bother collecting a loser's medal and if Offiah is about to move then he can go if that's the kind of attitude he intends displaying.

second half they played substan-

Offiah snub

SILK CUT CHALLENGE CUP 1993 FINAL

WIDNES v WIGAN

WEMBLEY

When Widnes lost the 1991 Premiership Final against Hull the question was asked by Paul Cook in the *WWN* "End of an era?". It wasn't, but it was after the loss to Wigan in the 1993 Challenge Cup Final.

Fixtures, results, attendances and points scorers 1992/93 season

Opposition	Venue	Result	Attend.	Goals	Tries
AUGUST					
30 Castleford	Home	16- 6	6,271	Davies (2)	D. Hulme, Goulding, Eyres
SEPTEMBER					
4 Hull Kingston Rovers	Away	16- 2	3,471	Davies (2)	Eyres (2), McCurrie
13 Carlisle (Lancashire Cup 1)	Home	52- 8	3,700	Davies (8)	Spruce (2), P. Hulme (2), Davies, McCurrie, Howard, Hadley, Currier
20 Bradford Northern	Home	12-24	5,365	Davies (2)	Eyres, D. Hulme
25 Wigan	Away	2-14	13,312	Davies	
30 St Helens (Lancashire Cup 2)		8-10	12,573	Davies (2)	McCurrie
OCTOBER					
4 Hull Kingston Rovers	Home	52- 0	4,700	Davies (8)	Devereux (4), Spruce (2), Davies, McCurrie, Hadley
11 Castleford	Away	14-28	5,998	Davies (3)	Holliday, Myers
18 Halifax	Home	20- 6	3,875	Devereux (4)	Devereux, Myler, P. Hulme
NOVEMBER					
1 Leeds	Away	16-48	12,040	Davies (2)	McCurrie, Hadley, Eyres
8 York (Regal Trophy 1)	Home	46- 4	3,343	Davies (7)	Holliday (2), Moriarty (2), O'Neill (2), Wright, Myers
13 Wigan	Home	6-18	6,326	Goulding	D. Hulme
22 Sheffield Eagles	Away	30-32	3,676	Currler (2), Goulding	Currier (3), Goulding, Eyres, Spruce
DECEMBER					
1 Wakefield Trinity	Home	16-10	3,960	Goulding (2)	Devereux (2), O'Neill
8 Rochdale Hornets (Regal Trophy 2)	Home	30- 2	3,591	Goulding (3)	Myers (2), Moriarty, P. Hulme, Koloto, Currier
29 Bradford Northern (Regal Trophy 3)	Away	10-21	5,346	Currier	Koloto, Devereux
JANUARY					
6 Salford	Away	48-12	3,513	Davies (6)	Devereux (2), Eyres, O'Neill, Spruce, Currier, Sorensen P. Hulme, Hadley
10 Hull	Away	4-20	4,562		Eyres
13 Swinton (Challenge Cup preliminary)	Home	62-14	2,154	Davies (6)	Koloto (3), Davies (2), Howard (2), Spruce (2), Currier, D. Hulme, Sorensen
17 Sheffield Eagles	Home	56-10	4,220	Davies (10)	Davies (3), Wright (2), Eyres, Currier, Koloto, Moriarty
20 Warrington	Away	10- 8	5,832	Davies	Currier, Wright
31 Whitehaven (Challenge Cup 1)	Away	20- 8	4,440	Davies (2)	Devereux (2), Currier, Myers
FEBRUARY					
7 Hull	Home	22- 4	4,594	Davies (3)	Currier, Davies, Faimalo, Sarsfield
14 Sheffield Eagles (Challenge Cup 2)	Away	52- 6	2,760	Davies (3), Goulding (3)	Currier (2), Davies (2), Wright (2) Devereux (2) Spruce (2)
17 St Helens	Home	26- 8	8,700	Davies (5)	Currier, Marsh, Moriarty, Wright
21 Wakefield Trinity	Away	36-18	4,330	Davies (4)	Moriarty (2), Davies, Devereux, Howard, McCurrie, Spruce
28 Hull Kingston Rovers (Challenge Cup 3)	Away	4- 4	6,286		Spruce
MARCH					
3 Hull Kingston Rovers (Challenge Cup 3 replay)	Home	16-11	7,095	Davies (4)	Eyres, Howard
13 Leeds (Challenge Cup semi)	Wigan	39- 4	13,823	Davies (5), Goulding dg	Davies (2), Myers (2), Currier, Devereux, Spruce
17 Leeds	Home	19- 8	6,482	Davies (3), Goulding dg	Devereux, McCurrie, Myers
21 Leigh	Away	14-11	5,069	Tyrer (3)	Devereux, P. Hulme
26 Salford	Home	38-22	4,109	Davies (5)	Devereux (2), D. Hulme (2), Goulding, Eyres, Myers
31 Bradford Northern	Away	0-28	3,536	-	-
APRIL					
4 Halifax	Away	6-40	6,011	Davies	Eyres
9 Warrington	Home	26-14	6,125	Davies (3)	McCurrie (3), D. Hulme, Myers
12 St Helens	Away	18-29	11,947	Davies (3)	Holliday, Myers, Spruce
18 Leigh	Home	26-28	4,989	Tyrer (2) Currier	Myers (2), Currier, Faimalo, McCurrie
25 Leeds (Premiership 1)	Home	10-22	6,554	Davies	Davies, Devereux
MAY					
1 Wigan (Challenge Cup Final)	Wembley	14-20	77,684	Davies (3)	Eyres, Sorensen

Players total number of games and points 1992/93 season

	Played	Goals	Tries	Points
Andy Currier	27	4	16	72
Paul Davidson	7			0
Jonathan Davies	30	106	14	268
John Devereux	33		21	84
Barry Dowd	1			0
Richie Eyres	35		13	52
Esene Famialo	30		2	8
Bobby Goulding	33	(2dgs) 14	3	42
Adrian Hadley	20		4	16
Karle Hammond	3			0
Les Holliday	25		4	16
Harvey Howard	34		5	20
David Hulme	35		7	28
Paul Hulme	33		6	24
Andy Ireland	2			0
Chris Kelly	1			0
Emosi Koloto	17		6	24
David Marsh	3		1	4
Steve McCurrie	30		11	44
Paul Moriarty	29		7	28
David Myers	27		13	52
Tony Myler	6		1	4
Jules O'Neill	12		4	16
Steve Pickett	1			0
Mark Sarsfield	4		1	4
David Smith	2			0
Kurt Sorensen	29		3	12
Stuart Spruce	14		2	8
Christian Tyrer	6			0
Darren Wright	31		7	28

First Division	Games	Won	Drawn	Lost	For	Against	Points
Wigan	26	20	1	5	744	327	41
St Helens	26	15	1	5	632	345	41
Bradford Northern	26	15	0	11	553	334	30
Widnes	**26**	**15**	**0**	**11**	**549**	**446**	**30**
Leeds	26	14	2	10	595	522	30
Castleford	26	14	1	11	544	401	29
Halifax	26	13	0	13	557	505	26
Warrington	26	12	1	13	487	450	25
Hull	26	10	1	15	381	535	21
Sheffield Eagles	26	10	1	15	405	627	21
Leigh	26	9	2	15	410	630	20
Wakefield Trinity	26	8	2	16	405	535	18
Salford	26	9	0	17	498	725	18
Hull Kingston Rovers	26	7	0	19	321	599	14

THE BIG THREE: Kurt, Doug and Martin at the dinner commemorating the 25th anniversary of the 1989 World Club Championship victory.

Lightning Source UK Ltd.
Milton Keynes UK
UKHW020815241221
396123UK00003B/21

9 781909 465